8 Pounds of Butter and Cheese

Letters from the Civil War by
Ira S. Jeffers 137th N.Y.V.

by

Eugene Mongello

authorHOUSE®

AuthorHouse™
1663 Liberty Drive, Suite 200
Bloomington, IN 47403
www.authorhouse.com
Phone: 1-800-839-8640

First published by AuthorHouse   6/13/2008

ISBN: 978-1-4343-7542-1 (sc)

Printed in the United States of America
Bloomington, Indiana

This book is printed on acid-free paper.

1) Copies of letters from Charlie English and David Cleutz

2) Original letters at The U.S. Army Military Institute at Carlisle Barracks in Pennsylvania

3) Original letter at The Museum of Virginia

A special thanks to Robert Walker Jr. and Anthony Caldropoli for all their help with this book.

Ira S. Jeffers
October 28, 1843 – March 13, 1932

" Grandfather told me to be a good boy and not
desert, tell him that I will not stain my name by
deserting. Tell him that he shall have one grandson
that he may feel proud of....one that I hope is a true
patriot who rather perish fighting for his country
than live a long life with a dishonest name"

Ira S. Jeffers
April 5th, 1863

The 137th, New York Volunteer's

The 137th NYV's were organized in Binghamton, New York. Captain David Ireland, of the 15th United States Infantry was given authority to recruit this regiment. At that time he was promoted to Colonel. Four companies were raised in Broome, three in Tioga, and three in Tompkins Counties. Recruiting started on August 15, 1862, and the full regiment being mustered into service on September 25th. Two days later, with 1,008 men they left for Harper's Ferry.

Little is needed to be said of the departure of the regiment, for similar scenes were at that time occurring in many cities and towns all over the country. When the boys marched from their camps to the railroads for transportation to the war, cheers and applause were given to these brave volunteer soldiers as they marched through the streets.

The 137th NY was originally part of The Twelfth Corps, Third Brigade, Second Division of The Army of the Potomac. Their first experience was in and around Harper's Ferry, Charlestown, and Winchester Virginia. They suffered through the hardships of General Ambrose E. Burnside's "Mud March" and saw severe action during the Battles of Chancellorsville and on Culp's Hill in Gettysburg Pa. The casualties for the 137th NY at Gettysburg were 40 killed, 87 wounded and 10 missing.

The Twelfth Corps. left Virginia in September, 1863 and went to Tennessee joining the Army of The Cumberland. In the following month the 137th NY engaged in the midnight battle at Wauhatchie, Tennessee. The casualties for that battle were 15 killed and 75 wounded. A few weeks later the 137th NY fought along side with General Hooker at Lookout Mountain in the famous "Battle Above the Clouds". Again the 137th NY sustained heavy loses, 6 killed, 32 wounded.

In April, 1864 The Twelfth Corps. was reassigned to The Twentieth Corps. under the command of General Hooker, with Colonel Ireland retaining his command. During The Atlanta Campaign they fought at such places as Rocky Face Ridge, and Resaca, where Colonel Ireland was wounded. They move on to Dallas, Kenesaw Mountain, Pine Mountain, Marietta Road, Peach Tree Creek, and in the trenches of Atlanta itself. On September 10, 1864 during the occupation of Atlanta, Colonel Ireland dies after a painful bout with dysentery, and his body is sent back home to Binghamton.

On November 15, 1864, the 137th NY left Atlanta and accompanied General William T. Sherman on his infamous "March to the Sea". This ended with the capture of the Port of Savannah on December 22, of that year. In the spring they marched north through the Carolina's. After a successful two month campaign, General Joseph E. Johnson surrendered his forces to General Sherman on April 26, 1865.

For Ira S. Jeffers and the rest of the men of the 137th NY, the war is finally over. But it came with a bloody price. The total casualties for the 137th NY were: 122 killed, 243 wounded, and 75 missing. Ira S Jeffers was no different then the other tens of thousands of soldiers, North or South. He never led a gallant charge, or received any metal for bravery. He did what was expected of him, and was proud to serve his country. The letters you are about to read are exactly how he wrote them, poor grammar, misspelled words, and run on sentences.

1862

Harper's Ferry Virginia, September 27 – 30
Duty at Bolivar Heights until December
Reconnaissance to Rippon Virginia, November 9
Charlestown, November 9
Reconnaissance to Winchester, December 2 – 6
Charlestown and Berryville, December 2
March to Fredericksburg Virginia, December 9 -16

1) The first page from Ira S. Jeffers diary

Saturday Sept. 27th 1862
left Binghamton at noon   got off from the cars at Elmira
and marched through the streets until dark   got onto the
cars again.

Sunday the 28th
run all night and all day got to Baltomore at dark. Marched
through the city took the cars for Washington

Monday the 29th
got to Washington at day light. stopped and rested. started
for the heights and got part way across the Potomac river and
receved different orders and come back to Washington. left
our knap sacks and took the cars for Fredricek City.

Tuesday the 30th
got to the city and went to the camp

Wensday Oct. 1th
in camp all day

Thursday 2th
in camp all day

Friday 3th
took the cars to Sandy Hook. got here in the eveing

1) Washington D.C.
Sept. 29 1862

Dear Parents

Having for the first time a few moments of my own i took the opporttunity to write. we are at Washington we expect to go to Harpers Ferry in the morning but are not certain were we shall go. I am well and hearty. I saw John Vanname this moring tell Albert i have seen the White House and lots of steam boats and other vessels   i can buy paper as cheap hear as in Binghamton   apples are worth 3 and 4 cents   i have had a plenty to eat yet i have eat two days rations in one day. It is some warmer here than it is to home but i do not feel the heat much   the ground is red like iron ore and the boys are about the same color   i have not much to write today but as soon as i get settled i will write a good long one You need not write until i write again   some of the boys say we are going to Fredrick.

This from Your Son
Ira S. Jeffers

1) Fredrick City
Oct. 1 1862

Dear Parents

In about ten minuts after i wrote to you at Washington we were ordered to this city. we do not know how long we are a going to stay. I saw Cap. Tracy regiment at Annapoles junction and they said they a comming here. we have bread and raw pork. some times we put it on a stick and let the grease drop on the bread and it tasts better to me now than it did to home fried in the sfder. we have coffee for breakfast and some times crackers for supper. I have had nothing but bread to eat some of the time. last night is the first night that i have not rode in the all night. It agrees with me yet to sleep on the ground i have not felt better in a year than since i left Binghamton. This city is full of soldiers you can not look any where around it without seeing camps almost as far as you can see. Stonewall Jackson is supposed to be some where not fur from Harpers Ferry. some say we are within 20 miles of Harper Ferry. out letters are forwarded.
Direct to Ira S. Jeffers
Washington D.C.   Co. F   137 Reg.
Kanes Brigade

Dear Parents

   We have had quite a gaunt since i left home but i stand it well   i have not been sick a moment since i left Binghamton we are at Harpers Ferry on the Potomac river. we expect to go into Harpers ferry soon. we are on a Mountain where there has been some fighting   i slept on the ground last night without enny tent over me or enny thing under me. i can not write any more now for i expect to have to go on guard duty i have writen twice before   i dont know wether you have got them or not.

This from your Son
Ira S. Jeffers

Harpers Ferry by moon light

Camp Pleasant Valley, Maryland
Oct. 9th 1862

We moved from Sandy Hook the day i wrote to you. this valley is full of troops   Burnsides forces are here within a half mile of here. some of the boys are a going to see the 89th today. they cannot get but a few passes at a time and i shall have to wait till my turn comes. i have seen Charles Carman yesterday   we are within about a mile of Harpers Ferry   there is a mountain between us and the Ferry   they have had battles all around here.   here is where they had Jackson surrounded and then let him go it is reported that he is near here and our men on the heights are a going to shell him   we hear cannons every day or two   the boys have found shells balls and other things around here where there has been fighting we do not have much chance to run around our side of the camp so i cant write much interesting but i know you want to hear from me as often as you can so i will do the best i can. the boys some time think that we will have a fight in a short time because there are so many forces here but if we do i think we will be kept as reserves   but i do not think we will see much fighting. i have heard that the president has been to try and settle with the south. i heard that they wanted to make peace but you know more than i do likely about that. about our fare some of the time pretty good and some of the time prety tough   we have had bacon and pilot bread in the morning and coffee   at noon we have rice or beans and pork that is bacon   at night we have about the same as breakfast. we live verry well now to what we have done   we sleep on the ground most of the time   some times we get straw   i got some straw last night   i have not got any of the things that i brought from home but my silk hankerchief and one cotton and the rest of my things are in my knap sack at Washington. i do not want you to send me enny things for i shall not carry half of my things that is in my knap sack if i get them   i am well and have been all of since i come away   i want to as often as you can i want to hear from all of the folks Direct letters to 137 Regt.   In care of Col. David Ireland.

Your Son Ira

Camp Pleasant Valley
Oct. 10th 1862

Dear Parents

I receved your letter last night and lost no time in answering it. i am well and was glad to hear the same from you   i got a letter as soon as enny of the boys and felt like a little boy with a new cent   i wrote a letter to you in the morning and got yours at night but i will write now   i left my paper in my knap sack but expect to get it today. you may send me some stamps if you will and the envelope but nothing else for i have got more than i can carry now. i have not seen a sick day since i was at Binghamton but i have seen a good deal of the country since i left and i have seen some big guns   i see one gun that they said was a going on to the moniters that was about 4 or 5 feet through at the butt. tell Albert that they have Chestnuts here the same as we do and they have a other kind that grows on bushs with small burrs and only that is about as large as a bean and looks like a little acorn   tell Catherine i would not care if i had some of them pies and resk it or piece of bread and butter. i have not had enny butter since i left Binghamton nor enny bread since i left Washington. it has been hard crackers and bacon   we make some improvements in cooking   we fry our crackers and meat together and put some water in to soke them so they will fry   some of the boys grow poor and some grow fat i think i am flesher than i was when i come away   i think that if i was to come home i should be to lazy to work or enny thing else. i would not cared if grandfather had found me for i think i came rather short before i got to Washington   i got off the cars before i got to Harrisburg sunday the next day after we left Binghamton and went to a house to buy something to eat and an old lady gave me a whole pie and i think it tasted good and i saw some quinces on a tree and thought they were apples and the cars started to go i got a copple and run to the cars before i tasted of them i soon found out they were not apples.

This from your Son
Ira S. Jeffers

1) Camp Pleasent Valley, Maryland
Oct. 11th 1862

As it is a little cloudy today and sprinkles a little we have not had any rain yet   it is very warm days and very cold nights. our clothes do not look quite as nice as they did when we left home. the dirt is red like iron ore and shows like grease on our close. you must tell grandma that i have not give up yet but that i shall come back   i have just seen George Stringham   his health is very good now   Charles Stringham is at Washington sick. tell Father that bob says he wishes he was back a pulling stumps   i wish i could get my likeness taken and send it home to you   i have had my hair cut tight all over my head so i look bully   i have been talking with george a few monments and he says i have done as well to enlist were i have as any where there is.   some of the boys from the 89th a coming in now and most all the time and get through so as to see them. i dont suppose you can read this very well but i have not a very good place to write. i suppose Catherine will see a good many words spelt wrong but if you get the meaning that is enough. i have not much to write often if there is not much a going on   you can find time i guess to write one letter where i write two. all most every one has a different direction but if you send in care of Capt. Shipman i guess that will come stright.

This from your Son
Ira S. Jeffers

Camp Pleasant Valley
Oct. 12th 1862

Dear Parents

I am well and hope this will find you all the same i have got in the notion of writeing often and hope you will do the same i have not wrote to enny one else but you yet i have seen Charles Printice and Warren Vandenburg   they both look well   it has not been but a short time since they have had a battle and Charley had a ball put through his pants just below his knee and another through the seat of his pants without touching him. you have heard likely before this time that John Vanname has resined   we have heard heavy fireing today but do not know for certain how it has come out   we heard that our men had whiped them out and took 3 hundred prisoners but we can not belive what we hear half of the time   we enjoy ourselves first rate   Bob Winner and anouther fellow just like him are the life of the company but he thinks he had a little rather be a pulling stumps but it does not make much difference where he is   we have not got our knap sacks yet but expect them every day. i had to leave my letter for you to attend service   it has just began to rain quite smarty. we have had much rain i have had to buy my paper and envelopes and stamps i have paper and envelops enough when they get here   i wish you to send some stamps you must tell the folks that i am the same fellow that i was when i went away and that i am a coming home again when they get sick of me whitch i think will be about three years. there is 7 of us in a tent   Edger Elhuell and Bill Smith and Hiram Bullock are in the same tent that i am in. i dont know but i shall write to Lew Sepfield if i get time and i get my paper   there is no card playing a going on in camp and swearing is to be stoped or they will be courtmartial   the boys have got to look out now on how they talk   the agaitant Mr. Robert Wimmer says he thinks he will not call us out on dress parade on the account of the rain   we are jokeing and caring on so we cant half write and i think i shall have to put up my writeing for this time.   you must write often for it seems as if i had seen you   you must remember i am a good ways from home and a word from you is better that a good meal of vittules.

From Ira Jeffers to
Sophrona Jeffers

Direct to Ira S. Jeffers
Washington D.C.   Co. F.   137 N.Y. Vol   in care of Capt. Shipman

Dear Parents

I recived your letter on the eveing of the 16   i am well
but i have not been in enny battle   they had a battle withen
hearing of us yesterday but i have not heard how they came
out yet   i wrote to Lewis the other day and yesterday morning
i wrote to Aunt Malvina   i have written five or six letters
to you before this one   i have not seen Capt. Shipman to
speak to him since i got your letter but he has to sleep on
the ground as well as the rest of us for boards is something
we cannot get. we had a heavy rain last night but we did
not get wet. you may think that this is level land here but
you do not know enny thing about hills and mountains till
you come down this way   the land is a nice soil and is not
stony only where there is rocks   the mountains are a most all
rocks   they do not farm it as we do. they plough with four
mules and a wooden plough with and just cut and cover   it
looks as if it was plowed with a shovel plow   in some places
they have plows like white folks. in the place where we are
camped there has been a camp before and they took wheat
in the bundle for to lay on and when we come we burnt up
the old straw and i should think we burnt as much as ten
bushel of wheat that they had wasted. there is a stack of
wheat and two stacks of rye here now   they tie there horses
to it and let them eat what are a mind to of it. but they will
not let us have enny of it for to lay on   we get Hemlock
bows for bedding   you may think we turn tough well we do
but at home when i had everything nice sometimes i felt or
though i wanted something a little better   then i buy me
some cakes or pie   ginger cookies are a cent a piece   pie cost

20 to 25 cents but i do not buy much tobaco is one dollar a plug fine cut   a three cent paper for five cents   when we get into winter quarters if we do get in enny we shall send home for a box of things but if you should send enny thing now it aint likely we should get it   i have paper enough and i can get envelopes for a cent a piece   i wrote a spell ago for some stamps but likely you will get the letter before you get this   i would write more if i had enny thing to write   i will write more as soon as i can find enny thing to write about

From Ira Jeffers to his mother
you must write often i will do the
same

Camp Pleasant Valley
Oct 20th 1862

Dear Parents

I am well and hope you are all well   i have not had enny letters from enny body else but you yet   i have had two from you dated the 5th and one dated the 12th   this will not go out till tomorrow at 10 o'clock   i do not want to wait for sunday to write   it is very cool nights here and warm days   we have heavy fogs nights   i went down to the river and washed yesterday and i expect a pass tomorrow   if i get one i shall go and see the boys in the 89th Regt. if they have not moved   i have not herd from them in a day or two.   Capt. Shipman says he has not forgot his old friends   he says he has wrote three or four letters but they have not been finished   he says he will write one soon and have it printed.   i wish you would send me a paper once in a while when there is enny thing worth reading   it is not very thickly settled through where we have been only near the citys   the houses are mostley small log houses and block houses   sometimes you will see nice brick and framed houses   there is a good many stone houses   they are about half of them deserted   the corn grows a good deal taller here than it does at home.   cheese is 25 cents a pound   tobaco one dollar   cider 16 dollars a barrel and it is not often they can get enny   mackeral 18 dollars a barrel about 15 cents a piece for honey   50 cents a pound for bloona sargages 25 cents a pound   ink 10 cents a bottle and other things about the same   so you can see how soldiers money goes.   i have seen boys that started with 10 dollars that have not a dollar left   i have paid more for presents for the officers than i have used   i had 4 dollars when i left Binghamton and i have got two dollars left   i do not think i have been very extruvagent. i laid aside my letter a spell to see the boys for the 89th Almon Morris is here now Charles Amsbury has got back Morris says he would like why i did not enlist in there Company if i can get a pass i shall go up and see the boys than i will write again write often and i will do the same i shall write often whether you do or not tell Albert he must eat a piece of pie once in a while for me and tell Catherine if somebody does not come to our house for peaches before i get home i shall be mistaken.

From Ira S. Jeffers to his
Mother

1) Camp Pleasant Valley
Oct 20th 1862

Dear Parents

I dated my letter of sunday wrong   i think but it will not make much   difference   i am well   i have been up to the 89th Regt. today   i see Charles Amsbury and good many other boys that i know   Dick Downs is color bearer   he took the place of a fellow that was killed at the   battle of south Mountain   he looks just the same as he always did   he did not know me at first but he was glad to see me when he found out who i was   Charles Sringham is sick at Washington yet he has got the fever and also Georges health is good now   he was very sick when he was at Hatterus. i will have to put up my letter now for it is about bed time   i will finish in the morning so good night.

Oct 21 1862

we had a heavy frost last night   i dont see as it is enny warmer here than it is to home   we got some straw from the stack i told you about so we slept quite warm last night   it is so cold this morning that my fingers are so numb that i can hardly write   you may think we have lots of room here in our tent   they are about 3 feet high but we will have different ones this winter   i have heard that they have been drafting in New York state   i would like to know weather they are a going to. tell Albert he ought to be down here to gather black Walnuts there is enny amount of them   tell Wallace that i have not got A letter from him yet   i am a looking for one from Lewis soon and one from Aunt Malvinea   i wrote to them a quite a spell ago   i have got plenty of paper yet   i bought A dozen envelopes last night   i have not got enny stamps from you yet   i would like to have you send me the Repubilcan paper once in a while after you get through with it. we enjoy our selves first rate here   we heard that a flag of truce had gone through to Washington but weather it is so or not i cannot tell   i have not much to write so you must make as much of it as you can   i am well and tough as a bear.

Yours truly Ira S. Jeffers
to Sophona Jeffers

Direct to Ira S. Jeffers   Com. F 137Regt. N.Y.S. Vol.
Washington D.C. in care of Capt. Shipman

Pleasant Valley Near Harpers Ferry MD
Oct 22th 1862

I would like to hear from you as often as i can. i am not very well to day   i have got some cold and a slight touch of the disentary but i am not so sick but that i do full duty. i wrote a letter to uncle george yesterday   i shall look for a letter from you to night   i have not much to write now but i thought i would let you know how i was   i shall have to lay a side my letter to go on drill.

Oct 23th 1862

i did not get a chance to finish my letter yesterday. the disentary run me considerable yesterday after noon and last night. but it does not trouble me much to day   i think i shall be all right in a short time. i have not had it before since i left Binghamton. i dont know what kind of weather you have up north   it is prety cold nights now and high winds   i dont know as i told you about the frost we had   things looked quite white for a spell   i am excused from duty to day   i thought i would take it easy as long as i could just as well as not there is not enny news in picticular for me to write to day so i will close my letter   it is not a very long one but it will do to let you know how i am. you wanted i should write often when i write again i send you a view of Harpers ferry   i have not got but the two letters from you yet.

Direct as usual to
Ira S. Jeffers   Com F.
137reg. Ny.S.V.   Washington D.C.

Pleasant Valley near Harpers Ferry
Oct 24th 1862

Dear Parents

I paid 3 cents for this sheet of paper so you would have a idea of this place   i think John Brown ough to be hung for trying to get the niggers out of such a place   i am better today than i was yesterday   you may think i have not wrote how sick i was but i have not lied to you at all   i have just got a letter from Frealia   they are all well   i shall write to her as soon as i can   i got a letter from you last night and was glad to hear that all of the folks was well   i heard that the elmira post office was robbed on wensday night and Binghamton office on thursday night and the deposit office on friday night   i have not got a very good place to write. i have to set on the ground and i hold a bord in my lap so i had not ought to improve much in writeing   you must tell the boys that i have not forgot them but i have so many to write to that i cant get around to them all. i would like to all but i have to try and answer them all   i receved the stamps and envelopes all right   i had to buy my paper till i got my knap sack from Washington   i had paper enough in that to last till now   i have got 3 sheets left yet and i had some envelopes the other day i brought a dozen envelopes so i have enough for the present   the way we get ink is some of us go to the sutters and buys a bottle and that lasts one tent a good while i had to leave my letter for a spell for we had to fall in line very unexpectedly for inspection   it looks as though we were a going to move   i heard one of the Capt. Cooks tell another that he had orders to cook up three day rations ready for a march weather it is to fight or go into winter quarters i cannot tell   it may be only to Harpers Ferry   if we have to march a great ways you will not be likely to hear from me again very soon. i shall write when i can   tell Catherine i wish i could stuff my self with onions   you need not send enny more stamps till i write again   you asked why i did not write the boys   it was because i know how they was and did not think but what you know   Will Dodge is rather unwell as well as my self   Milton Knox is prety well   Bob Winner is a little aleing   it is the disentary that ales the boys   there is about 10 of our boys sick with it but they are so as to be around   one of our boys is so sick i think he will have to go to the hospital   them that are only a little sick dont go to the hospital only for there mediceen. i think i never wrote to you about John Wideman being sick   he was taken sick at Fredricek and was taken to the hospital and has been very sick   he is better now   he is out of the hospital now and begins to pick up his crumbs considerable.

Oct 25th 1862

I had to leave my letter for A drill and did not get A chance to finish yesterday   we have orders to stay in our company streets ready to march at enny moment   i do not know where we A going nor what we are A going to do   i shall not write A great deal this morning because i want to finish this time. you must write just the same when we are moveing as enny other time   the direction will be just the same   let us be where we will so good buy   tell Albert he must learn to write this winter so he can write to me next summer.

From your Son
Ira S. Jeffers

Direct to Ira S. Jeffers
Co. F 137 reg. N.Y.S.V.
Washington D.C.
Leave out the Kanes Brigade for we are not in that Brigade.

I received your letter on the evening of 27 and answered it as soon as i got a chance   it is evening now   i have to sit on the ground and hold my knapsack on my lap to write so i do not know whether i can write so you can read it or not but i guess you can. I am well and feel first rate   we fare very well now,   we have moved from where we was   we moved yesterday into virginia we passed through harpers ferry on our way here. and that letter i wrote to you with that picture on it is as perfect as can be. i was on guard the day and night before we started and so i did not get enny sleep till we got here in the middle of the after noon.   i can not write much to night on account of the position i have got to write in i wrote to you before i got this letter and wrote about the stamps   i got the things all write   you must tell Han that i will as soon as i get time i have not answered frelies letters yet i do not get as much time as i wish i had to write   Will Dode is well an so is milton Knox   there may be some times when i cant get time to write but i think i shall not forget to write. i have received all of the stamps you sent me   i forgot to mention it. i am always very carful when opening letters that nothing drops out   you must not show this to enny boddy for it is very poorly wrote and badly composed but i have not got no chance to do enny thing to night but i was bound to write enny how   if i wated till tomorrow it would not go out till next day   that little boy that was killed was a brother to this one that is with us   you wanted to know who done our cooking   some of the boys make a buisness of it   you do not do enny of the cooking unless it is put.   Harris have just got a letter from you and wallace and catherine   i have not got a no chance to answer it to night but i will tomorrow if i can get a chance   i wrote a letter to uncle lew a long time ago but you say nothing about it so i guess he has not got it   i got another piece of paper from you but have not read it yet   i will have to close my letter   i could not think of nothing to night   you must read this the best you can so good night.

From Ira S. Jeffers
to his Mother

Direct to
Ira S Jeffers   Com F
137 NYSV washington DC

I receved your letter dated the 26 in due time and was glad to hear from you all   i am well and hope you are all the same   tell Wallace that i write to him as soon as i can but i have not had time to answer Frealies letter yet   i did not get a chance to write to you the next day after i got your letter for we had to move again   we are now on the heights back think it is verry likely we shall stay a quite a spell for the old troops is a moving off   things look rough here you can pick up loaded guns and cartrages and good shoes and hats caps knives forks cups platters enny thing almost that a soldier has but it is verry little such trash that i pick up and what i do i shall leave when we move again   if i had some of these guns to home that is a kicking around here they would be worth something i wish you could just look into our camp here   it dont dont look like home camp   we are a rusty looking set but we stand it well   this company has got the least sick of enny   you have got that letter likely with the picture on   if you have you can see verry near where we are camped   it is back of the village between the two rivers   i dont know as you can hardly read this for i have got a poor place to write   you told about it freezing up there   it froze here ice as thick as window glass. we have had some heavy frosts here   you must tell Wallace not to be in enny hurry about getting a married. he might better wate till the war is over and tell Kate she had better write to me than enny other fellow if i ant quite as good looking. i have just got a letter from Uncle George and one from Lind and Juna   they say they have not heard from you since i left and Aunt Lind said she had not got that likeness yet and wanted to know where i had left it Uncle George gave me some good advice and i hope he has gave it to some one that will try and profit by it. tell Albert i would like to have his pig here to roast. i have not much more room so i will have to stop writeing i will write as often as i can but when we are a moveing so much i cant get time i would like to write four times a week if i could you must give my respects to Han and all of the rest of the folks tell Nor Macorley i have not heard enny thing from his boys yet.

Ira S. Jeffers

1) Boliver Height   Nov 10th 1862

I receved your letter a saterday eveing and one from uncle Lewis   i am well and was glad to hear that you was all well. i do not get as much time to write now as i did but i will write as often as i can   i have to be on guard or picket about every other day and when i am off i want to rest   yesterday the rebels got up as far as Charlestown and we went down there and drove them back   our Artillery shelled them from one piece of woods to another hill.   they drove them as far as they wanted to   the infantry was not engaged at all we formed in line of battle at Charlestown and marched about five miles acrossed   over lots of corn fields and fences and through the woods but the rebels run so that we could not get sight of them. General Segel and his flying Dutchman as the rebels call them were there   when we got to Charlestown we went into the houses and arrested about a hundred of the inhabitants and shut them up and when we found enny thing we wanted we took it   i got about two dollars worth of tobaco and could got more but did not want to be bothered to carry it. i think we got six horses and a colt and what pigs we was a mind to kill   one boy got 10 dollars worth of envelopes and stamps but i was not luckly enough to find enny of them   one of the darkeys got a box of tobaco and sold it to one of the sutlers for about 7 dollars   tell father i will try and pay the postage on the paper and am very glad he has signed for it   you was telling about it stormed   it puts me in mind of our snow storm. a friday morning it began to snow and snowed almost all day   the snow got to be about 3 inches deep   you must tell Han that i cannot get a chance to write her so she must read these when she wants to hear from me   tell her that the needle book is almost as full as it was when i got it   i can darn socks just as well as enny body tell Catherine to tell Mr. Scott that he must write me and tell him if he was down here with his washing machine he could make a lot of money. when you write to me send an envelope with stamp on and a sheet of paper   i lent a dollar of my money so i am short of stamps and paper   you need not send enny money unless i write for it   i can see where the money goes i dont think you will catch me short again i can get money if i was a suffering   tell Albert i wish he was down here a spell   he would not think we was the same fellows that he saw on Camp Susquehana   i shall have to leave my letter now and go on drill i have to leave my letter about 3 or 4 times before i can get it finished.

From Ira S. Jeffers

Bolvier Heights
Nov. 14th 1862

Dear Father and Mother

I receved your letter dated the 6 last eveing and was glad to hear from you   i have got two papers from Binghamton and a standard paper from Uncle Lewis   you must not expect that i can write a letter just as you would for i never wrote enny till i came down here   i mean to write to you all just as much as if i directed it to you all.   my health is good it is been better i think that it will average in the regiment   tell Catherine she must be contented with reading this because i have to leave my letter two or three times before i can get one finished.   we have not drawn our money yet but as soon as we do i will send it home   you see the letter in the paper so you know all about our marches   the other day when company a was out on picket they had three men taken prisoners by the rebels and i heard that our Pickets was fired on last night.   the rebels have been seen from this place   our men are cutting down the woods in the valley so the rebels will not have no place to crawl up to us with out being seen.   we have to be in readiness to be called out at enny moment   a good manny of the boys think we will be sent home in the spring   they think the war will be settled by that time but there is a good manny think it will not be settled by fighting.   there has five died in the regiment and i dont know how manny have been sent to the general hospital but there has been two from this company and more that ought to be.   David Durand was one that was sent off   we like our Captain verry well   he is full of fun and makes a good deal of noise but if we was a going into battle i should rather he would stay behind for he is no milatary man at all   we like our Leutenant first rate   when we went out before the cornel left the Captain to see to the camp   but the captain says next time he shall go enny how. tell Catherine it will not hurt her to write if i do not answer her letters   Will Dodge has been sick but he is better now he was not so sick but what he was around   Bob is the same fellow that he was when he came away only he dont sing as much as he did. Direct as useal.

Ira

Dear father and mother

I receved your letter the 18th but i just came in from picket and was very tired and sleepy and the next day i had had to work   so i did not get a chance to write till today   i am well as useal but there is a good many sick   there was one man burried this morning. there has 7 died in the Reg. but none from this company   you spoke about Capt. Eldrage being dead   i do not know whether he is or not   i heard that he was left at the hospital sick with the fever again and have not heard enny thing about him since   you must not think because i wrote so manny letters on the start and delay answering them now it is because i am negligent for it   it is because i cannot get the time   i could at first   we are now where we have got something to do   tell Grandmother that my socks is prety good yet   i have got 3 pair. them that she gave me i have not worn enny till now since we left Binghamton. i wrote to you in my other letter about stamps and paper   the lice are getting prety thick in camp especily body lice. i have not got enny of them yet   i am prety careful about catching them   my pen does not write very good so i will try a pencil   tell father to write and let me know what he thinks about the war ending in the spring. i dont know much about it but i think i shall be home to help him pull stumps next summer   it is not very cold here now   it rains a little here every day or two just enough to make it muddy Peter Hauver has got his discharge and is a going home in a day or two   you must tell bill if he gets Betty and wants to sell his share of the machine to wate till i get home and i will trade him my bounty land for it so he can have a snug little

farm of his own and be a Southern gentleman. tell Mr. Scott
i was very glad to hear from him but as i can not get time to
write he must read the letter that i write home   i have got to
hurry and get reddy for inspection so i shall have to quite.

From Ira S. Jeffers
to his Mother

Boliver Heights
Nov. 30th 1862

Dear Father and Mother

I have not heard from you in a long time or have not got my paper this week i am well and harty it has been quite a spell since i wrote so i thought that i would write today. i shall not get a chance to write very often now for they are building two or three forts and i have to go and chop every day but Sunday and if they get in a hurry i shall have to go Sunday there is a good many sick ones here with the measels. one man has died in this Company since i wrote to you his name is Corneius Cranell from Colesville Will Dodge health is prety good now he is fleshing up considerable Bob Winner health is just as good now as it was when he was at home we have not drawed our pay yet we may draw it in a short time and we may not draw it until spring they are calling us to turn out to atten a meeting so i shall have to stop writeing for a spell i shall get a chance to finish it to night.

Eveing Nov. 30th

I have not got but a few moments to write so i must hurry up if i get a letter from you soon i will try and answer it but shall have to write in the eveing unless i wait till Sunday. Milton Knox i think is just comeing down with the Measels he has been complaining a little for a day or to and tonight he is quite sick but if he gets very sick i will try and write to you i have been bothered so i cant write half what i wanted to but i guess i have wrote all of the news when you write be sure and send me paper and stamps i have got two or three envelopes yet tell Mr. Scott to write to me as often as he can if i do not write to him he can read your letter.
From Ira S. Jeffers
to his Mother

Boliver Heights Va   Dec 7th 1862

Dear Parents

I recived a letter from you the first of this month dated the 25th and another last night dated the 21th and was glad to hear that you was all well   my health is good. Milt Knox is better   he has the measels. we had to march to winchester we started the 2 and got back 6 with out loosing a man from this regt. and we took some prisoness but i dont know how many. i was on picket one night while we was gone and the rebel easerly fired on our men on a post just below where i was and then run but did not hit a man and then they came around back of our post and we fired on them and then they left. and the next day about two hundred caverly attacked our caverly of about 60 men but as soon as our cannon began to throw the shells they left. i think there is nothing much around here but few caverly i think the most of them have gone on to richmond. you may tell grandmother that She need not be afraid of my being homesick as long as my health is good as it is now   i dont know but i should be homesick if i was sick   my cloths are good there is not enny holes in them yet   they have riped some but i have mended them so they are as good as new   i have not had enny new cloths but an overcoat   i lost my first one   my socks are pretty good yet i have kept them darned up good but when i want enny new ones i can get them here but if mr doges folks have not sent will his box you might put in a couple of pair of socks for they ware better then goverment socks. milt has got a box from home and i got a pair of gloves in it and i got something to eat out of it two. father sent me a pair and they sent milt a pair and they got here in the right time for it has snowed and turned round very cold   you wanted to know how i stood the long marches   we have not had but two long marches yet but i stand first rate and being on picket is nothing but fun. you need not be afraid that i will not write the truth to you for i shall do just as i agreed to   milts measels have turned and he is quite smart   he did not have to go to the hospital at all and he said he was going to write home to day. i see in the papers that bill was married   you must tell him that i wish him much joy   i have just got a letter from fretia. i recived the envelopes and stamps and paper all right   Bob winner has got the ear ache prety bad other ways all the boys that you know is well   there was a fire in Harpers ferry last night and i heard it burnt up two stores. we have been out twice and the captain did not go nether time.

From Ira Jeffers To His Mother

Tell Bill i want him to come down here and live on my farm rent free

Fairfax   Dec 13th 1862

Dear Parents

I thought i would write and let you know where we are about. i have not had A chance to send a letter before since we left Bolívar Heights. i am well and feel first rate only i am prety tired to night. we have had some prety hard marching and expect some more. i do not know where we are a going only we are a going on towards richmond. Our forces occupy Fredricksburg they have taken it since we started. we will probably go as far as alaxandra tomorrow and there we may take the cars and we may not. the army is in motion now and there will be a battle some where near Richmond before you get this I think. our company is some smaller than it was when we left Binghamton   there has two died and one discharged and i think two disserted and one is Oscar Nowlan   we have got 52 men with us and the rest are sick in the Hospital. milton Knox is with us he has got over the measles but in not quite got his strength back yet. you may not hear from me again in a good while for we may be where we can not send them but i will do the best i can

From Ira S. Jeffers
To His Mother

cap shipman is with
us this time

tell Melissa i
will look for
george in alaxandra

Part of the Medical Report from Surgeon John M. Farrington 137th NYV on the conditions of Bolivar Heights, Va.

December 14, 1862

The regiment went to Bolivar Heights November 1, 1862. The site of the camp had been continuously occupied by Union or Confederate troops from the very beginning of the war. The result was that the soil, saturated with the germs of disease, made our camp a pestilential one. Soon we were visited with a grave and extensive epidemic of typhoid fever, and our regimental sick list increased rapidly until it reached 200. It became necessary to sent the most severe cases to the general hospital at Harper's Ferry, where on one day, four of our men died from the disease. During the last four weeks of our stay at Bolivar heights there were nearly 400 cases of typhoid fever, and scarcely a day passes without a death in camp. On December 10, with 650 pale, jaundiced, and enfeebled men we left 110 men in camp who were to feeble to march, and who were transferred from there to the general hospital after the regiment had left. The remaining survivors of the regiment were absent, sick in hospital, or had been discharged from service direct from the general hospital. So depressing had been the influence of our pestilential camp that there was scarcely a well man in the regiment, but on the march, with better surroundings, the health of the regiment rapidly improved.

Dr. John M. Farrington
Surgeon, 137th NYV.

Camp near Fairfax Station
Dec. 21th 1862

Dear Parents

I receved a letter from you last night dated the 4th and was glad to hear from you again i have not had a chance to get enny letters before since we left Harpers Ferry for we have been on the march about ten days we marched about as far as Dumfries and then marched back as far as this station i do not know how long we shall stay where here. we expect every moment to have orders to march some where i stand the marching first rate my health is good i wrote to you when we was at Fairfax that our men had got Fredricksburg but it was not to be i suppose Burnside is badly whipped that is the report now and i suppose that is why we fell back but i cant tell much about it i have receved your envelopes and stamps all right and i want you to send every time when you can and be sure that the envelopes have good sealing on them i cannot write to you very often when we are on the march and if i could i may be where i could send them. i have not wrote to enny boddy in a good while but you only one letter to Jamese King he wrote to me and Will. he wanted i should do as i agreed to and write to him Milt is about as well as ever he was not able to carry his knapsack on the marching but he stood the march first rate and has got a good appitite now.

Dear Kate

I thought i would write a few lines to you this time being you do so well i think you gain finely a writeing if you keep on you will get so in a short time you will do all the writeing. you tell about haveing bully times at school i think we are haveing bully here. i wish you could just see us now and see us cook i can beat you a cooking the boys say that i am getting fat i think i ought to i am sure i could eat enough i wish i could see Wallace a short time i think i could tell him some prety tall storys and if he had got a stomache stronger that a horse i would be apt to turn it i make some of them gag here once in a while. tell father that Charles Stow the Supertendant of the railroad from Fairfax Station to Washington was here in camp yesterday and Capt. Shipman went down to the station and made him a visit this is is the Stow that married Bob Smiths sister i think i heard mother speak of him i have not got my two last papers yet but shall probly get them soon and there must be some later letters that i have not but letters that have been writen a long time seen new i have not much news to write today but i have managed to fill out my paper with something. Milt has wrote for a new diary and one for Luke and so i told him to send for one for me and have them all come together and i would pay him for it. you need not send me enny money till i write for it.

From Ira S. Jeffers
to his Sister and
Parents

Camp near Fairfax Station
Christmas morning Dec. 25 1862

Dear Parents

I just receved your letter of the 12th and was glad to hear from you again   i have just come in from picket and Milt has just gone out and i and Luke are just a going to have a good Christmas dinner of fried beef and soft bread. you dont know what hard bread is but if i ever send some home or come home i will bring some to you and when you talk about fat beef i wish you could see some that we kill here. we kill them to save there lives and i think it a pity to throw away the hides for they are about half or two thirds taned by the time they get them off but occasonly we get a good fat one. we have got a bully good piece for dinner   we fare very well now   we have good salt pork about every third day and the other two days beef. we have all the coffee we want and a spoon full of sugar a day and once in a while A ration of tea and when we are in camp we generily get soft bread half the time which is plenty often enough for the hard bread goes rather farther than the soft bread. when we are in camp we live well enough but when we are on the march we see some prety tough times. the talk is now of going into winter quarter some where for three months   it will proably be so muddy that they cant do much till then   it is quite warm here now for this time of the year but i suppose it is cooler up north. the Captain thinks we shall draw our pay next month so you must look for the letters for i shall send home my money as soon as i get it   we shall probaly drew 4 months pay which will come very acceptable to the most of us especily men that has got familys. there has been conciderable dissattisfaction among them for not getting it sooner and threaten to desert as soon as they get it. there has quite a number deserted from the regiment already and two from our company   Corperal Nowlan and Sergent O.W. Emmonds both of them officers but the Capt. says he is glad they are have gone and the company is as well suited as it is. i have heard a good manny of the old regiment talk prety strong of desertion they dont like the style of thing is a going on but let them desert that wants to i dont think if you wate to see me till i desert you will not probably see me very soon for i came with the intentions of staying till was honerably discharged and i am very confident that i shall do it   there is some all the time growling because they are not used better and them are the ones that are are sure to be homesick but there are mostly all in prety good spirts   you spoke about prices of things they are some higher here Butter 50 cents a lb. Cheese 25 cents a pound Blolona saurage 30 cents Cookies 3 for 5 cents and tobaco i dont know about what the price is. i have got a small piece left yet of what i got in Charlestown   i could give away enny amount if i had it but every one has to look for himself here first. i have not much news to write today but i have filled up the paper with some things   so no more at Present.

From Ira S. Jeffers
to his Parents

ps Bob says tell Lev to tell Bill to look for the Animel. please let us know if Bill Lectures to his Scholars.

1863

"Mud March" January 20 -24
Fairfax Station until April 27

Chancellor Campaign April 27 – May 6
Battle of Chancellorsville, May 1 – 5

Gettysburg Campaign June 11 – July 24
Battle of Gettysburg, July 1 – 3
Pursuit of General Lee to Manassas Gap Virginia, July 5 – 24
Duty on the line of the Rappahannock until September
Movement to Bridgeport Alabama, September 24 – October 4
Reopening the Tennessee River, October 26 – 29
Battle of Wauhatchie Tennessee, October 28 – 29

Chattanooga-Ringgold Campaign November 23 – 27
Lookout Mountain, November 23 – 24
Mission Ridge, November 25
Ringgold Gap, Taylor's Ridge, November 27

cover of a piece of woods and support the artillery for our Regt. was in the advance and by the time we had got into line the shells were flying pretty fast after the retreating Rebs. we lay in the woods a short time and then our company was sent out as pickets. we stayed out about a half an hour and then was ordered on to our Regt. which had gone on and we had to double quick it and catch up and then our company was sent out as skirmishers that is to advance a head through the woods in line 4 paces apart and see what we can find but we got into a kind of swamp and when the order was given to halt only eleven of the company heard it and the rest of us went on about half a mile and then we thought something was wrong so we halted and found out that some of our men was missing so we lay there about half a hour until one of our caverly men found us and took us back to our Regt. we got catched up with them about dark found the rest of the company all right but they had given us up as goners they thought we was all taken prisoners we halted that night within about 5 or 6 miles of Dumfries our caverly went to Dumfries that night and found our forces there but they had one days hard fighting and lost some men. they brought back two dead men and two wounded ones that they found in the woods the next day we started back for this camp and got here Tuesday noon all right only we was prety hungry for our teamsters heard that we was retreating so they turned back and got into camp as soon as they could and left us without enny thing to eat. it is News Years day today i wish you all a happy new year it is quite pleasent here today my health is good i stood the march well. Milt has got well he carried his knapsack this time the Capt. did not go with us for he was down to the station when we left we have been mustered again for pay but i do not know whether we will get it very soon or not but i think likely enough we shall have to wate a quite a spell yet and if father has got the money so he can i wish he could send me a couple dollars but if he has not the money to spare he need not send but one. i have got out of tobaco and i would like the money   i have not borrowed enny money till this morning   i got 50 cents from Milt write to the boys and have them send Milt and me a diary when they send one to Knox. i am sorry that i did not bring one for the last year for then i could tell where i was every day and what i done. i know one thing we done   we went prety hungry but i happened to have rather more crackers that the rest and i got some persimmons for my dinner one day comeing back   they are a kind of wild fruit that grow in trees   they look like plumes   when they get ripe they are very sweet   some of the boys would keep watch along the road where we had stopped to eat and pick up all the crumbs and once in A while they would find quite a piece of cracker but then when we got into camp there general filled up. Pete Wents has got the Small Pox at Alaxandra.

From Ira S. Jeffers
to his Parents

1)Camp near Fairfax Station
Jan. 7th 1863

Dear Parents

I receved your letter dated the 30th night before last but did not get a chance to write till today for we are a drilling or on inspection every day. it is a beautiful sight to see us all out on inspection   on the ground were there is about 10 thousand men drilling at once   my health is good   i have had a slight cold but got nearly over it now   Bob Winner and Will Dodge are both well   i think Bobs health is as good here as it was at home   i have heard that Thomas Knowland has moved back on to the hill again   if he has will you will be likely to see Oscar before long and if you do i want you to let me know what he says about soldiering.

Jan. 8th 1863

I did not have time to finish my letter yesterday so i will try and finish now. i have not much to write this time but i know you wanted to hear from me often as you could   i get my paper every week and Milt get his   there was one of the boys in Company A fell down today and his gun went off and shot off two of this fingers   there is nothing for me to write so i will wate till next time there is sufirerent to let you know how i am and next time i write i will try and write a longer one.

From Ira S. Jeffers
to his Parents

Camp near Fairfax Station
Jan. 16th 1863

Dear Parents

I have not receved a letter from you since i wrote to you i think likely there is one on the way some where   we are under marching orders now expecting to march every day so i though i would while i had time. my health is good   i had the sick head ache the other night but i took a good cleaning out with Mandrake so i am all right now   our regiment looks prety small now   there has a good many died and there is a great many sick in the hospitals now   there has been quite a number deserted   the first night after we got our orders to be ready to march there was 14 deserted and last night 10 more left and i dont know how many more will go to night. Capt. Eldrage got here yesterday   he looks as tough as ever Ed Elwell has just come back   he left the Regt. to go to the hospital at Harper Ferry. i have not had a chance to talk with him yet   i spoke about our regiment looking small   you can judge something how it looks your self   we had 1024 men when we left Binghamton and now we dont muster more than 400 men fit for duty   Gen. Geary came out and gave the regiment a good talking to for deserting this morning which will probably check them some for a spell. three of the men that deserted night before last deserted from picket post and i heard that one of them had been picked up and if he has he will probably be shot   for it is different whether they desert their post of camp   there has not but 5 deserted from our company yet and there was 5 from company K deserted in one night   but i did not come here to desert nor i dont intend to and above all to desert my post or in the face of the enemy. i heard by way of one of the boys that my conduct in the skirmish near Dumfries was highly spoken of by the officers and and he said i was one of the best soldiers. i have been on every march yet and as long as i have my health as good as it has been i shall stick by them   we have not had our pay yet and dont know when we shall get it   if we start off on a march we wont get it very soon but if we stay here i think we shall get it soon. some think that if we move from here that we will go to Newbern N.C. for it is getting so muddy that they cant go much moveing the artilley and other think we are going to Fredicksburg. but we dont know were they intend to send us. no more at present.

Ira S. Jeffers

Aquira Landing
Jan. 26 1863

Dear Parents

I receved a letter from you the 23 and was glad to hear that you were all well   my health is good   there is not much sickness in camp now.   we have marched 7 days and got to Aquira Landing where we expect to stay a spell as guard   but do not know how long   we may   stay two months and we may not stay two days   we got here yesterday.   Mr. Knox came down to see the boys and got there the day before we started from Fairfax Station and went back the next day.   he brought me and Milt and Luke a diary apiece so i can tell what we have done every day.   the Captain is a going home on a visit if we stay here a spell and if he does i want Father to go and see him.   i got my money all right and am much abiged to Father for sending it   i have got all the clothing that i want we drew all the clothing we wanted at Fairfax and i dont want enny box sent for i might not get it till it had spoiled   i got my paper dated the 14th   they do not get here till they have been printed about a week   they get here sooner if we are in camp   George Dolittle came down with Mr. Knox and he stayed and marched with us but is going back soon.   we expect our pay within a day or two if we stay here but they say we will not get but two months pay now.

Ira S. Jeffers

I did not get a chance to finish my letter till today   the Paymaster came here yesterday and paid off two companys and paid off the rest of us today. he only paid us from the time we enlisted up to the first of November. so i only got 17 dollars and 33 cents   they say that they will be around again in a short time. i lost my overcoat when we was on Boliver Heights and i could not drew one then so i had to buy one i bought it off the Liutenant and was to pay him 5 dollars for it when i got my pay and i have paid him and every body else that i owed enny thing. and some of the boys was owen me so i have settled up with them all and will have 5 dollars left after i send you the 10 dollar check you will find in the letter. i am i hope to send you more next time. i got my last weeks paper whitch had Capt. Shipmans letter in it   the wind blows so hard that i cant write much now and i have got to fix up my tent so no more at present.

From Ira S. Jeffers
to his Parents

i got the money father sent me all right i got it the 23 day of Jan. and am much obliged to father for it. we got our pay the 30th yesthey only paid us from the time of enlisting up to the first of November but the paymaster said that we would be paid again in about 20 days. i got 17 dollars and 33 cents and sent you a ten dollar cheek and paid my dets and have got 5 dollars left. you wanted to know about Bugdorf it was the boy that died. he went to the Hospital before we left harpers ferry he had the feaver and Jet Briggs i dont know where he is i have not seen him in a long time. Will dodge got his Box before we left Fairfax station and it was in good condition, and if you want to send me a box you may send a small one, one that will weigh about 50 pounds or if miss

Dodge wants to send one to Will

you might send one together and if you do send one i would like to have you send it as soon as you can so i can get it while we are here. my clothes are good we got new clothes at Fairfax but if you send a box grandmother may send a couple pair of socks. and you may send six or 8 pounds of Butter and about as much Cheese if you can get it and some pepper and a couple tins of buiscuit and plenty of cakes and if you send enny pie put plenty of paper between then and if you have got enny sausage or dried Beef send some of that. there aint much use of my telling you what to send for you know about as well as i can tell you only dont put in enny thing to dampen the Box enny more than you can help ther has been a number of Boxes spoilt by putting

53

Acquia Landing
Feb 1 1863

I recivied your letter the 30th dated the 22 and had just writen one and got it sealed up but as i had time to day i thought i would write again. my health is good and Will and Bob are both well. we are guarding the railroad and working on the dock unloading government stores. they detail 15 men from each company to work on the dock for 10 days they go to work before daylight and dont get back till dark. so when it comes my turn i shall not get a chance to write in 10 days unless i get some of the boys to work in my place when i want to write whitch i guess i can. we have hard Bread pork coffee sugar and some of the time Beans and rice and some of the time freash beef. i got the money father sent me all right i got it the 23 day of Jan. and am much olbiged to father for it. we got our pay the 30th they only paid us from the time of inlisting up to the first of November but the pay master said that we would be paid again in about 20 days. i got 17 dollors and 33 cents and sent you a ten dollor check and paid my dets and have got 5 dollors left. you wanted to know about Bugdorf he was the boy that died he went to the Hospital before we left harpers ferry he had the fever and Jet Brigs i dont know where he is i have not seen him in a long time. Will dodge got his Box before we left fairfax station and it was in good condition. and if you want to send me a box you may send a small one. one that will weigh about 50 pounds or if miss Dodge wants to send one to will you might send one together and if you do send one i would like to have you send it as soon as you can so i can get it while we are here. my clothes are good we got new clothes at fairfax but if you send a box grandmother may send a couple pair of socks. and you may sent six or 8 pounds of Butter and about as much Cheese if you can get it and some pepper and a couple tins of biscuits and plenty of cakes and if you send enny pie put plenty of paper Between them and if you have got enny sausage or dried Beef send some of that. there aint much use of my telling you what to send for you know about as well as i can tell you only dont put in enny thing to dampen the Box enny more then you can help there has been a number of Boxes spoiled by putting in Chickens. you want to put in plenty of paper around the pies. you may send what you are a mind and if you think it wont pay to send a Box you need not sent it. i will send you two dollors to pay the freight if you send it. i dont want to have so much money here at a time i will keep 3 dollors and when i want more i will send for it.

i wrote a letter to grandfather Scofield yesterday i do not get much time to write and when i do have time i dont write to enny body but you for if i wrote to one i would have to write to another or they would think they were slighted. tell mr. Dun that i was glad to hear from him and to hear that he is getting better. tell Catherine next time she writes to get a new Pen.

from Ira S. Jeffers
to his Parents
Direct a box the same as a letter

Acquia Landing Feb 5th 1863

Dear Parents

I recived your letter Dated the 29th yesterday. and one from uncle george day before yesterday they are getting along very well now. they said that they had not heard from you since you was up there. my health is good and Will Dodge is well but Bob is not as well as usial. the captain says he has got the Chronic Diarhea but he is so as to be around. there is about 64 men in our company now. it is the largest company in the regiment and i think the best. the names of them that has died is Cornelas Crannell David Monroe James Burghdorf Luther Frink Smith Howe Zerah Spaulding and Corporal Riley W. Hine and the sick in general Hospitals are S. Matterson George Youngs John Egelstone Wilsey Spaulding Oliver Tuttle William Jenks Malon Pardee Eli Watrous Sherman Watrous Perry Wines Hamilton VanNess John Wilcox Corporal Marvine D Matoon Brundage Welton Robert Cresson and David Durand if he aint Deserted. and the Deserted is sergent O.W. Emmonds Corporal O.F. Nowland Pat Harriss George Hanter and one Deserted and was gone two days and then came back and said that he did not start to Desert he only went out to see the Pickets and got lost but i am prety shure he intenended to Desert. by the way he left his things but we have the least Deserted from our company than enny other company in the regiment. i think our company wares the Belle and when you talk about my Deserting it will when my mind a great deal different from what it has been yet. i would rather die on the field of Battle. life is but short at the best and if i live to come home i want to look people in the face and not be ashamed of myself. i dont think that if i deserted i would be thought quite as much of by the people in our place as i was before i came away. i have got the money you sent all right and have just got 10 sheets of paper but have not got enny stamps or envelopes. it is so cold that i cant write much more now for my fingers are so numb that i can hardely hold my pen.

Afternoon Feb 5th

it has snowed most all day but now it has turned to rain and i think it will be a rainy night. it is not quite as pleasant to be in nothing but shelter tents in such storms as it to be in a house with a good fire but you cant expect it to be as pleasant here in virginia mud. you dont know nothing about mud up north you ought to see us on a march when we go into the mud half way up to our knees. and see the artillery move the small 12 pounder guns whitch 6 horses would trot off with on a good road get stuck with 12 horses and then it is fun to be driver on bagage wagons you will see as manny as a dozen mules down at a time and one get killed every little while but nobody cares for they belong to uncle Sam. but i think uncle Sam has got to be prety rich to keep up such a war as this. but if he can stand it i can.

Ira S. Jeffers
Acquia landing Va.

Aquira Landing
Feb 17 1863

Dear Parents

I recived your letter this morning dated the 11th and had no time in answering it. you did not say ennything about the checks nor the two dollors that i send so i think you had not got it when you wrote but have got likely before this time. i sent the check the 30th of Jan. and about the box i am much oblige to you for trying to send me one and tell magrett Han and the rest of the folks that i thank them for their good intentions. i think i am not quite forgotton yet. i dont care so much about the box as i do the way the other soldiers do about such things. i think they want us to patronize the sutles but what they make out of me they are welcome to. i will name the prices of some of the things a two quart tin pail with cover they ask 10 shillings. some of the boys wanted to buy them for to boil coffee in but they dont sell many and many tobaco from 10 to 12 shillings a plug but i went on to a boat down to the landing and bought a plug for a dollor but if the officers found out that enny one was selling enny thing to the soldiers for enny thing near what it was worth they would shut them up or something else   Butter 50 cents per pound   cheese 30   apples 4 for ten cents   cookies 2 cents apiece   fried cakes 2 cents apiece   pies 25 cents with 3 pieces of apples and a crust just right for leather aprons   led pencils 10 cents and other things in propotion and stamps. i dont know how much they do have to pay for i have not bought enny. you must tell miss McSorley that i am much obliged to her for the stamps. and i would like to know whether she has heard from her boys lately or not and where they are. i suppose you think we have prety nice weather down here in

Va but about the kind we have   here is it will be warm as summer one day and the next it will be cold enough to take the hair off from a yallor dog. it was very pleasant yesterday but to day it has snowed till it is about 4 inches deep and is snowing yet and when it gets through snowing it will rain or melt off and then the mud will be hub deep   we are haveing our worst weather now. i am glad that we aint a marching now although we had as bad a time on our last march   it is not likely we shall again very soon. you said you send some things by the Captain   i dont want you to send enny thing only if you are and mind to send me a good jack knife i would like it   i would like one with two blades but dont send enny medicen   i got all the medicen i want.

A few lines to Sister Kate

Being enny of the rest of the boys wont write to you i will. my health is good as ever and i am as tough as a bear   i guess you would think i was if you could see me   i have been down on the dock to work eleven nights right along. and i dont know how many nights more i shall have to before they put me on day detail but they will keep us to `work. the 9 army corps has gone down to north Carolina   the 89 regt was among them   i saw leutanant morriss and leutanant Armsburg   the rest of the boys that i knew had gone on board the boat before i got down to the landing. if you can find my gold pen if it is good for enny thing i wish you would send it in the next letter you write

Aquira Landing   March 8 1863

Dear Parents

I receved your letter dated March 1st on the 6th but i was out on picket and did not have a chance to write till i came into camp today. i can not write much this time for i am not very well   i have got a very hard cold and the Doctor has given me some medicen and says that i must go to bed and cover up warm and be still the rest of the day. Bob Winner is at home likely before this time. i got your letter dated the 19 of Feb. and commenced to answer it but never could get it finished for they kept us to work all of the time. i cannot write enny more this afternoon but i will write again in a few days and answer al of your questions. i got Wallace and Kates letter.

I . S. Jeffers

Aquira Landing   March 10th

Dear Parents.

I wrote a few lines to you the 8th. just enough to let you know how i was and that i had recived your letter. yesterday i was so weak that i could not sit up much of the time but i am a good deal better to day. i shall be all right in a day or two. i think i should had a turn of the feaver but the Doctor gave me some medicen that broke it up right along. you wanted to know how many there is in my tent and who they are. there is six of us William H. Green   George Dolittle Horrace Nickolas   William W. Wheeler   Allison Aimsworth. they have brought Pat Harriss back again   he is over to Gen Geary head quarters. he came here to the company yesterday under guard to see some of the boys but they were most all away to work. he looked rather sorrowful. i guess he wished he had stayed here. you have seen bob before this time likely and have heard from me and heard all about what is going on in camp. i shall not write much to day for my hand trembles so that it is hard work so no more. i will write again if i am enny worst. i will answer grandfather as soon as i get it and write some to you at the same time

I. S. Jeffers

it is a small letter so i will send a small envelope

Dear Grandparents

I receved your letter dated 5th today and was very sorry to hear that your health has not been as good as usual. i am not getting well very fast just now but i am getting better   i had got the Drerea and had a hard cold together. we have got good log tents with fire places and good bunks made of poles and covered with hay and corn stocks so we sleep first rate   our shelter tents makes a good roof and our tent is just large enough to hold six of us comfortably so there is quite a snug little family of us when we are all at home. you have seen Bob Winner probably before this time and heard from all of the boys   they are all the same as when they went away to work all of the time.

From your Grandson
Ira S. Jeffers

Winter camp

Dear Parents

I feel very well this morning only i have not got much of
an appatite but i got some dried berries off one of the boys
and cooked them and when they get cool i guess i can make
quite a breakfast out of them. the boys are all getting boxs
again   a man by the name of Scovill from Binghamton had
a box shipped the 5th of March and got it the 11th. that
came through in a short time   you will probably have my
box started before you get this letter   i receved the pens in
the other letter all right but you had better not send the gold
one   i want to know if Father has seen the Captain yet and
what did he say about me   Bob will tell you just as things
are but the Captain has got so much gass about him that you
cant belive half he says. i will write again soon and let you
know how i am getting along.

I. S. Jeffers

March 16th 1863

Dear Parents

    I though that i would write a few lines to you to let you know how i am getting along. i am very weak but feel quite well other wise the Doctors said that i came very near having the fever. i have grown quite poor but i should have been poorer if i had the fever one of the men in our company cut his foot today very bad he cut off one of his toes and cut the rest so that the Doctors had to cut two more he will be likely to get his discharged Will Dodge is as fat as a bear he went up the railroad yesterday 6 or 8 miles to see the 27th regt. and has not got back yet he will be back this afternoon some time. i dont feel like writeing much this time so i will wate till i get one from you before i write again.

                Ira S. Jeffers

Letter from home to Ira Jeffers

Binghamton
March 15th 1863

My son, we are all well as usual. We got your
letter of the 8th and the one of the 10th and I was
sorry to hear you were sick but was glad to hear
that you was getting better. I hope you will be
well again before this reaches you. Mr. Shioman
starts for the south tomorrow, your father went
and saw him and got a knife for you and has
sent it by the Captain and one pair of socks and
a towel. The knife is a white handle with two
blades and it cost six shillings. We have not
seen Bob yet, he has not been at home much, he
has been down to Gill Hasbrooks the most of the
time. So we have not heard anything from him
only that he said that you was well and getting
fat. Grandma sent the towel and the socks to
you. Likely you have got the letter I wrote for
your Grandma and Grandpa before this time.
Grandma is very much concerned about you for
fear that you are a going to be sick, she thinks
that you have not wrote how sick you was. But I
think that you would not write anything but the
truth about it. It has been very unsteady weather
here this winter and there has been a great deal
of sickness everywhere. There is a great many die
with the sore throat called Dypthera. Uncle Alva
has been quite sick with it, he is better now. Your
father and I went down there last Thursday to
see him. School is out and they had an exibition
last Wednesday night and it was first rate one.
Catherine had a part in a piece called The
Sewing Society. It all went off without a single

break down. Little Deal Printice came out on the stage and sung "Colonel Elsworth Revenge" and was not embarrassed in the least. Mr. Scott was well pleased with the exibition, there was a very full house. And it was very still so it went off very well. I saw Charley Printice there, he is home on a furlough for a few days, he said that he had seen you twice and you looked fat and tough. Shipman said that you cooked and eat and was as tough as a pig. I shall write to you as often as I get a letter from you and perhaps oftener, you must write as often as you can and if you are not well enough to write get some of the boys to write for you. If you should be very sick let us know and your father I think would come and see you.

This from Sophrona S. Jeffers
to Ira Jeffers

p.s. I send you an envelope and stamps if you want more than one stamp at a time let me know. Albert says that he shall not write you again till you say one word to him. When you want paper let me know.

I received your letter to day dated the 15 and was glad to hear that you are all well. i feel quite well but i am very weak the Doctor comes to see me every morning so i dont go out only when i am obliged to whitch is not very often. i can sit up or lie in my bunk so i am as comfortable as you please. we have got tents made of logs and our shelter tents for the roof and a good fire place so it is warm and pleasant. it has snowed most all day but it melts about as fast as it comes. Pat Harriss has got back   i have seen him twice they say that he asked cornel Ireland to take him back to the regiment and the cornel told him that he did not want him   that he had no room for such men. the captain got back last wensday and i got my things all right. tell father that he sent me just such a knife as i wanted. tell grandma that i thank her very much for the things she sent me. and i got their letter the 11th. and i got a letter from frelia yesterday but i have not answered it yet. tell grandma not to worry about my being sick for i am getting better and i will write just how sick i be. if i cant write there is enough of the boys that will write for me. i got the envelope and stamp and wafer all right. i have got 4 sheets of paper yet and 7 envelopes and one stamp that frelia sent me. you can send paper or i will buy it here i think you could send a package cheaper that i can buy it here you can send 12 sheets of paper and 12 envelopes and a letter all in the same envelope for about 15 cents get a large envelope to send it in. that is what it cost to send such a one to one of the boys in our tent.

March 21th

it is a snowing again to day   it snowed nearly all day yesterday but it melted about as fast as it came and i guess it will turn to rain to day. i feel better to day then i did yesterday. the captain gave me some dried apples and some peach pickles and some crackers and some butter so that i have got some thing that i can eat i have had soft Bread all of the time since i have been sick and sugar and butter but i had to buy my butter at the sutters. i have had enough to eat since i have been sick when i have had enny appitie to eat. i have wanted pickles and such things. the sutter had Cucumber pickles in quart bottles and he asked 60 cents a bottle for them but i thought i could not afford to pay so much so i done with out them. i did not know but i might get a box. but you did not say enny thing about it in your letter so i dont suppose you have started one yet. you must tell Albert that he must look out that little mike dont kick him for i think he would kick harder than an old musket and they kick hard enough. i suppose that you know that Milt Knox is a corporal.

Ira S. Jeffers

March 26th 1863

Dear Parents

I am getting about well again   the Doctor dont give me enny more medicen   he says that i dont need enny more he thinks all that i want now is a good appitite and plenty to eat and stay in my tent and keep quite till i get my strength again   i feel well so it is a hard job for me to keep still   so far as i could not find enny thing else to bring myself to do i thought i would write a letter. i can eat about as much now as ever so i think i shall be out soon   well they are expedting that there will be a battle at Fredricksburg in a short time General Hooker says that he will take the city or lose the last man that he has got. and it is reported that he has sent in a flag of truce and ordered the women and children all out of the city. he reviewed our Brigade the 19th of this month and it is said that we are under marching orders   but if they do have a battle we may not be in it for there is a good many troops between us and Fredricksburg. i dont think that we will leave this place in a good while yet and we may not leave here this summer unless they want to put new troops in here. we are getting to be what you might call old troops   it will soon be a year since we enlisted and we have been through just the same as the old soldiers. while the 109th has not been doing enny thing but guarding the railroad at Anaplolas Junction but they seem to getting tired of being still in one place so long. it is expected that there will be considerable hard fighting done in the next three months i think that the Rebs must begin to be prety well cornered by this time and if we are ever a going to whip them i dont see why we cant do it this spring as well as enny time. but if i was some Big

General i suppose i might know more about it   so i will not write about some thing that i dont know enny thing about so i will change the subject and inquire about how Mr. John Darling family is a getting along and how all the rest of the folks is. and tell Father i want him to write and let me know what he thinks about our new commander in Chief General Hooker or fighting Joe as a good many call him. i have wrote about all that i can think of so i guess that i shall have to stop i expect a letter from you in a day or two and i though that i would wate till i got it before i wrote but as i had time and wanted to do something i though it would not hurt me to write again so no more at present   let me know when you get this by answering it inmediatly.

From Ira S. Jeffers
To his Parents

A list of letters Recived and sent since the 23 of January.
Recived
23 a letter from home with 3 dollars
30 a letter from home

February
 2 a letter from G. C. Bishop
17 a letter from home
19 a letter from home
27 a letter from W W Scofield

March
6 a letter from home
11 a letter from grandfather Jeffers
19 a letter from Afrelia Collins
20 a letter from home

January sent
30th a letter with Check
31 a letter to grandfather Scofield

February
1 a letter home with two dollars
6 a letter home
6 a letter to G. C. Bishop
6 a letter to W. W. Scofield
16 a letter to Afrelia Collins
18 a letter home

March
1 a letter to W. W. Scofield
8 a letter home
10 a letter home
12 a letter to grandfather Jeffers
16 a letter home
21 a letter home
24 a letter to Afrelia Collins
26 a letter home
27 a letter to Malvina Hooper
29 a letter to Ira L. Scofield

and i have wrote one to Amander darling whitch i forgot to note down in the time of it but i think i wrote it about the 27th of February and have not recived an answer from it yet. those that let me wate so long for a answer i think i shall do the same with them after this. i want you should keep this list and about the first of may i will send you another. it is quite warm and pleasant to day   it is as warm as summer and our regiment is having a general inspection and i am in my tent writing. i am getting quite strong again   i shall be able to do duty again in a few days. i have not had a letter from you since the 20th but i got my box the 28th all right. but the box of peppers the cover got off from it and it was all over every thing but i dusted the things off so they was as good as ever but what a nice time we all had a sneezing for a spell. i wrote a letter to uncle Lew thanking him and Emiline for their presants.

Dear Parents

I dont get a letter from you yet   i think that you must have written one but it has got miscarried some way. i had ought to wrote again before this time but i expected that i would get one the next time that the male came in. but i would have wrote sooner if i had had enny stamps. i have borrowed one and shall have to borrow another to put on this one. General Slocum and green inspected our camp ground and tents to day. the 1st army corps left here about 6 weeks ago and went to newport news and the 25th of last month they were in Baltamore they took the Baltamore and Ohio railroad from tennasee where they were to be under there old commander General Burnside   that is the corps that the 89th regiment is in.

Acquia Landing
April 2/63

We recived two dispatches from Fredricksburg about three days ago that Fredricksburg was evacuated and our cavalry had been through there two or three times that day. we hear a great many camp rumers now. some think that we are going to Kentucky and others think that we will go to Washington to do provost duty or to fortress monroe and some think that we will stay here where we are but we dont know what we are a going to do. we have got a nice camp ground here for summer. it is on the top of a hill close to the Potomac where the Breeze blows cool. the river is about 6 miles wide here so you may judge some thing for your self about what kind of a place we have got. but it is not likely there will be much of a force left here this summer. it may be that we will be the ones that will stay here and it may not. but it dont make enny difference to us we had just as well go to Kentucky or not or enny where else. the more we travel the more we shall see   but dont think the war will last much longer. if they would let a fellow go home once in a while especily when he is sick i would about as live be here as enny where. it was rather tough at first for to be obelgated to do everything that these self concited pups with stripes on told you to. but they wanted to show their athority. but almost a year experience has learnt us all a good deal   one was that they could not make an entire slave of you. you see us on a march an officer then is no better then a private only as and an officer and when we have a good cool headed officer one that will not flinch when there is danger is not apt to be left alone. we have got one Commissioned officer that i would not turn my back upon as long as i am unhurt and able to follow him if it was through the heard of the rebellion. he is the one that has had command of us in nearly all our skimishing yet. he is from Windsor. i dont know but i might as well tell you his name. it is Leutenant W. N. Sage. but we are very well suited with our officers in our company and i dont think you could find a better Cornel or Leutenant Cornel. our Cornel is quite strict and wants to see his men all clean and neat as possible and their equitments all in good order so as to never be taken by surprise and to be ready for enny emergency.

April 3.

it is going to be a very warm today. and i am on light duty for the first time since the 8th of march. when i was sick i did not sense enny pain at all but i was so weak that i could not sit up but a short time at once. the doctor wanted that i should go to the Hospital but i told him that i had rather stay in my tent. one of the boys said that he would take care of me if he would let me stay. so he said if i did not get enny worst he would let me stay where i was.

Ira S. Jeffers

Acquia Landing
April 5th 1863

Dear Parents

I receved two letters yesterday one dated the 21th and the one from Kate dated the 29th in whitch she said Grandfather was very sick and was not expected to live. he told Catherine to tell me to be a good boy and not desert   if he yet lives tell him that i will not stain my name by deserting   tell him that he shall have one Grandson that he may feel proud of one that i hope is a true patriot who rather perish fighting for his country than live a long life with a dishonesed name but war is a terrible thing   it makes many homes desolate. the loss of a husband and father   the mother loses her son it may be her only child whom left his peaceful home to protect his country. i am getting smart again   i am so that i do light duty that is nothing but roll call and dress parade the Doctor did not put me on duty till i asked them to. they wont put me on full duty for some time yet   i dont think for they know that i am willing to do duty when i can. the weather is very unsteady now   it will be as warm as summer one day and the next day it will rain or snow   it commenced snowing last night about dark and snowed all night and it is nearly all melted off now so it is all splash. i want to know what father is going to do this summer. Catherine said that he had hired Wallace to work for him   tell Albert that i was glad that he sent me the pencil for it was just what i wanted tell Sarah Frier that i thank her very much for the presents and the box you sent for a pepper box   we dont have the use for one   one of the boys in our tent had a good one sent from home   the box suited me first rate and it was plenty large enough for this time of year   i read the price to the boys that you did not want i should make a pig of my self but remember that i was just a boy. then they laughed they said that they wished that you could see me eat but my apitite was for meat and the doctor said that he wanted i should eat all the Beef that i could eat and when we did not have beef he sent it to me from the hospital so i did not want enny of my cheese for two or three days after i got my box but the crackers was just what i wanted and i had soft bread. so i had bread and meat and crackers and butter and apple sauce and tea. so i lived first rate we draw tea once a week some of the time and we have all the coffee that we want to have we have got about six pounds of coffee on hand now and about a quarter of a pound of tea. we draw potatoes once a week and onions too. also sugar and beans we get a heaping table spoon full of sugar a day and 4 days ration of beef and 3 days ration of pork for a week 4 days ration of soft bread so you can see we eat very well now i shall have to stop writing for now for i have filled up my sheet send me six or 8 stamps next time if you have them so you can put a piece of paper around them or put them in a envelope all that you have sent me have come all right yet.

Ira S. Jeffers

Acquia Landing
April 11th 63

Dear Parents

I receved your letter this afternoon in whitch you said that Grandfather was dead but i heard of it before i got the letter   Bob winner got back this forenoon   he looks a great deal better then he did when he went away. he thinks that it is a good deal warmer here than it is up north. it is very warm here to day   if i was not for the cool breeze from the Potomac it would be as our summer weather at home   it is to warm for comfort now. i am as well as ever and i think better only i have not got quite as strong as i was before yet. but will be all right in a short time. we went up to Stafford Court House yesterday and was reviewed by President Lincoln with the rest of the 12th army corps and we went up and back the same day marching about 18 miles in all. the boys said that i was a going to tire out so they took my gun and carried it for me and the cornel came along and see that they was carring it so he asked me if i was sick and i told him what was the trouble with me and he said that if i would try and get up there he would let me ride back. i told him that i would after we had marched back about 3 miles. he was going past and he see me again and called me to come and get on his horse so I did.   so after i had got rested i rode up to him and told him that i could get along then but he told me to go ahead and after we had got within about 2 miles of camp he beconed to me to stop so i rode back to where he was and he gave me his sword to carry   i asked him if he had not rather ride but he said no so I rode to camp. but i was prety stiff this morning and we got all so tired that the cornel said that we might not get up till 7 o'clock in the morning. that was an hour later than the usial time. but about 10 o'clock this morning we heard heavy movement and several volleys of musketry and soon the orders came from head quarters for the men to be under arms imediately whitch was done with the excption of 3 or 4 men who run and hid and was hunted up and brought in at the point of the bayonet but they did not belong to our company. the boys said that i had better not go but i told them that i should go if they did. so they went and told the captain and he told me to fall out when they started and i thought they would be enough that would fall out with me so i told him that i should go as far as i could before i fell out. but we did not have to go   we was kept in line about an hour and then stacked our arms and went to our quarters but kept our straps on so as to be ready to fall in at a moments notice if the orders came to march till about two o'clock then we was dissmissed. we have not heard what the trouble was yet.

April 12th 1863

I have not heard what the fireing yesterday was for yet for certain. there is several different stories been told about it. i shall probably know before i write again

From your Son

Ira

ps i got the stamps all right

April 16th 1863

Dear Parents

    I have just come in from pickets and i though i would write a few lines to you while i had a chance for we have got marching orders. i do not know what moment we may be called on to go we have turned over a part of our clothing to the Quartermaster so that we can carry the more rations and we have got to carry eight days rations and our knapsacks with one pair of stockings one shirt one pair drawers one piece shelter tent one rubber blanket one woolen blanket and over coat. sixty rounds of cartrigers witch will make a prety good. we may go sooner and we may not go in two weeks they are fixing to make a grand move some were and as soon as the main army starts then we shall have to move on i have just seen Dick Downs i have not seen him since we left Pleasant Valley he was Color Bearer then in the 89th Regt. but he is in the regular Cavelry now. he is on his way to Washington after horses there is about 500 men of them in all a going after the horses. the Rebels hold Fredricksburg yet the weather is good here now it is nice summer weather only a heavy rain we had yesterday witch will probably detain them some about moveing but if it dont rain enny more it will not detain them long   i dont think that i can stand a very long march yet but i shall go as far as i can and when i give out they will have to put me in the ambulance. Pvt. Harriss has got back to the company i have not had enny thing to do with him   he dont have much to say to the boys or they to him   i guess he dont feel much better than he would if he had stayed here. the boys use him well when he does speak to them but they dont run after him   tell Wallace that i want that he should answer my last letter that i wrote to him or i wont write to him again very soon   i do not get many letters now   about all the letters i get come from home but if they dont answer my letters i shant write to them and write the more home. i have got 7 letters that aint answered besides what i have sent home but i know that you will write as often as you can.

This from your Son
Ira

April 17th 1863

Dear Sister

I will finish my letter this morning   there is nothing new to write   we have got our knapsacks all packed ready for a march as soon as they call for us   i am in hopes that they will not march quite yet.   you must write to me as often as you can   if i dont write to you as long as i write i write to Mother is it just the same   if you do not get a letter from me again very soon you need not think strange for if we march i may not get a chance to write but   will write as often as i can.

Ira S. Jeffers

Acquia Landing
April 19th 1863

Dear Parents

I receved your letter yesterday dated the 14th and was glad to here that you was all enjoying good health. I am about as tough as ever and am getting fat as a pig   we are under marching orders and have been for sometime   our knapsacks are all packed and our haversacks are all filled besides what hard tack we have cramped into our knapsacks and are to be kept so for we do not know what moment they will call on us   it is just as likely to be at midnight as enny other time but we are all ready but pulling down our tents. it is very pleasant weather here   now the grass has got started so that cattle could get quite a bite and the peach trees are all in full Bloom and have been for sometime. there is a nice large plantation not far from where we are in camp and a large orchard of peach   apple   quinces   cherry trees   and a nice flower garden and a many current and goose berry bushes

Troops waiting to move out

but it is deserted and the house is torn down or burnt up. i have not much to write to day so i will write short letters and write often. tell grandmother that my mustache is not very extinguish yet and i have had a good time smoking my cigar.

Ira S. Jeffers

Acquia Landing
April 24th 1863

Dear Parents

we have not marched yet   we are still on the old camp ground but our rations are kept packed ready to start. we have had nice summer weather for a couple of weeks back until yesterday morning then it began to rain and it is raining yet. i was on ordinance guard yesterday and last night   it was not very pleasant but i have got a good ruber blanket so i got along very well. we signed the pay roll yesterday and got our pay to day   i got 52 dollars. one check of 40 dollars and twelve dollars in money. i will send the check this time and when i write again i will send some more   i do not want to keep much money at a time. i had rather send home after it as i want it. we have got our pay now up to the first of march but we have got nearly two months pay due us yet. i receved a letter from uncle Lew yesterday but i dont get enny from wallace   i wrote a letter to him the first of march and have not receved an answer from him yet. i have not much to write this time and as i am going to write again soon you must make this do this time.

This from your
Affectionet Son Ira.

Acquia Landing Va.
April 26 1863

Dear Parents

I receved your letter yesterday dated the 20th and one from Afrelia Collins whitch i answered the same day and finished writing one to Uncle Lew. i have not receved a letter from John Darling yet but i will probably in time   we soon expect to start on a march   tomorrow maybe but we dont know for certain nor we dont know where they intend to go. we was inspected this morning by Cornel Irland and last wednesday by Brigadier General Green   the amabulance wagon came and took all of the sick to the general hospital this morning so that looks as though they intended to move soon   if we start on a march i shall not probably get much time to write   i should like to stay here for we have got such a nice place for a camp that it seems hard for to leave it   we cannot lie idle a great while   that is not what we came here for. there is a good many fish caught here   Shad Bass Eels Herron and all most enny kind that you could call for besides Oysters are found not far from here and kept at the landing all of the time   the landing is not very large place   there is no dwelling houses   there is all store houses Sutlers stores and such government buildings   it is about as large as it was when we came here. it has been burnt down twice since the war began once by our men and once by the Rebels. it is quite an important place   there is a railroad running from here to Fredrickburg and from there i dont know where it goes to   but it would bother the rebs some to get it   the boys catch a good many black snakes here now   they have just brough one in alive that is between 5 and 6 feet long   but i dont fancy them much they are to snaky for me   the idea of layin on the ground at night with a hugh black snake for a bed fellow   but them that are aquainted with them say that they are harmless. the Captain has just told the boys that the Adjuntant General has been here today and says that we are to march tomorrow. it is not likely that we shall stay here a great while enny way   i have got 11 dollars and a half left yet and that was for i only spent 50cents for Tobacco   i should have sent five dollars of it home to day if i could have got a ten dollar bill broke.

From Ira S. Jeffers
to his Parents

in Chickens. you want to put in
plenty of paper around the pies.
you may send what you
are a mind and if you think it
wont pay to send a box you need
not send it. i will send you two
dollars to pay the freight if you
send it and i dont want to have so
much money here at a time i will
keep 3 dollars and when i want more
i will send for it. i wrote a letter
to grandfather Scofield yesterday
I do not get much time to write
and when i do have time i dont
write to enny body but you for if
i wrote to one i would have to write to
another or they would think they were
slighted. tell mr Dunn that i was
glad to hear from him and to hear
that he getting better. tell Catherine
next time she writes to get a new
Pen. from Ira S Jeffers to his Parents

Direct a box the same
as a letter

Aquia Landing, Feb 1st 1863
I received your letter the 30th
dated the 22 and had just written
one and got it sealed up but as i
had time to day i thought i would
write again. my health is good and
Well and Bob are both well. we are
guarding the railroad and working on
the dock unloading government stores
they detail 15 men from each company to work on the dock for 10 days
they go to work before daylight and
dont get back till dark. so when it
comes my turn i shall not get a
chance to write in 10 days unless
i get some of the boys to work in
my place when i want to write
which i guess i can. we have
hard Bread pork coffee sugar and some
of the time Beanes and rice and
some of the time beash beef

May 8th 1863

Dear Parents

It has been some time since i have writen to you so i think you must be anxious to hear from me by this time. but it is the first time that i have had a chance to write or to send one since i wrote to you before we started on a march the 27th of April. went through by the way of Stafford Court House crossed the Rapahanock at Kelleys Ford the 29th crossed the Rapadana river the same night and took a number of Rebels that was at work there building a bridge. marched all day the next day. May the first the battle was commenced about 10 o'clock and lasted till dark mostly all Artillery fighting. that night we was nearly surounded and had to work nearly all night throwing up breast works of brush on dirt about all the tools we had to work with was our bayonets for picks and our tin plates for shovels but we all worked with a will for retreat was sure destruction. it was fight or die and it might be both. May 2nd saw fighting all day a great deal of Infantry engaged the fight was kept up nearly all night. Sunday the rebs flanked us in the morning and fired on us from both sides on the right compelling us to fall back from the fight to the entrenchments on the left. Monday 4th not much fireing today went out skirmishing to find the position of the rebs. found them in the woods within about a half a mile of our trench we returned back and went to work building entrenchments worked nearly all night. Tuesday 5th worked on entrenchments a part of the time rained very hard about dark. Wednesday 6th crossed the Rapahanock at United States Ford before day light halted for the night with in about 8 miles of Stafford Court House. Thursday 7th marched back to Acquia Creek. the results of the expedition is not fully explaned yet you will probaly know the results as soon as i do for i expect it was a great battle it is said to be the hardest battle that has been forth yet. our Regiment is said to have only 80 missing and wounded there is one missing in our company and one wounded slighly with a buck shot through the fleashly part of his arm the others are all right in our company. you will probably see the full account of the battle in the papers soon. the battlefield represents a horrible sight such as i hope will not be seen many times more. my health has never been better that it is now. tell Father he may send the paper six months longer if he will. i got a letter from John Darling yesterday and two from home. i dont think we shall stay here a great while i think we shall soon have to be moving again. so no more at present.

Ira S. Jeffers

Dear Sister

as i have not got much to do today i though i would write a few lines to your self individuly as so that you cannot have to say that i never write to you. i am well and tough as a bear i think that i have never felt better we had a prety tough time on this last march we had to carry 8 days rations besides our clothing and 60 rounds of cartriges after the first days march you could pick up enny amount of clothing i threw away my over coat and all the clothing i had only what i had on. only my rubber blanket and tent cloth whitch i lost on the battlefield on Sunday together with my knapsack at the time that we had to fall back from our entrenchments. the name of our battlefield was Chanslorville you probabaly have seen a full account of it in the papers before this time. i have not for they have not allowed enny New York papers here since we first started from Acquia nor enny other paper until last Saturday. then they let them bring in the Sunday morning Chronical whitch i belive is a Washington paper as near as i can learn the Rebels was prety well used up and our Cavelry raid between Fredricksburg and Richmond has cut off there supplies and communications between the two citys there is no use of my trying to discribe the looks of the battlefield. the men that came in when the battle was nearly over said that the ground was almost covered with dead and wounded. that was Sunday the day that we had to fall back from our entrenchments we fell back about a half a mile were we came to some fresh Artillery that had not been engaged yet when the Rebs came up our men opened on them with grape and canster cutting them down

by whole regiments at a time   then there was another corpse
of fresh troops took our place and we went into the woods
to rest and got some sleep and some thing to eat   but there
was no rest for us. we had hardley got our arms stacked and
commenced to build some fires to cook our coffee when they
commenced to shell us and finely to scatter some grape shot
amoung us compelling us to move our quarters as soon as
possable   the loss in our company is one wounded and one
missing   our regiment lay about two hours under a heavy
cross fire before we left our entrenchments and did not lose
but a few men. our Major was hit on the temple with a piece
of a shell whitch knocked him senceless but i have heard that
he was not seriously hurt.

I.S. Jeffers

Acquia Landing
May 14th 1863

Dear Parents

I receved your letter to day the 10th and lost no time in answering it i have writen one letter to you and one to Catherine since the battle. i did not get wounded there was only one wounded in our company and he was shot through the fleashly part of the arm with buck shot there is one missing that cannot be accounted for but they think he is killed. there is about 50 killed wounded and missing in our regiment i have heard a good many say that they though it was a merrical that we escaped with so small a loss. there was not much of our regiment engaged with musketry but we was under fire of shot and shells for three days nearly all of the time and a Sunday morning we lay under cross fire of the Rebs for about two hours with out haveing enny chance to return it whitch was not a very pleasant situation especilly as they had a company of sharp shooters laying in ambush to pick us off. you will see a letter in the Republican soon that will give a full account of the march and of the battle from Capt. H.W. Shipman. i suppose it was the greatest battle that there has been since the commencement of the war and i think will soon be followed up with another. inclosed you will find 10 dollars. i have been trying to get it changed so as to send part of it home but as i cant get it changed i will send the whole of it when i want some money i will write home for it as i do not want to keep so much here at a time i shall have two dollars left after sending you the 10 whitch will be all i shall want to use for some time for i dont buy much but tobacco whitch dont only cost 12 shillings a plug.

Ira S. Jeffers
Co. F 137 Regt. NYSV
3 Brigade 2 Divison
12th Army Corps

Acquia Landing
Sunday May 17th 1863

Dear Parents

I receved your letter today dated the 13th and as i have time this after noon to answer it i will not wate. although i have not much to write only to let you know that i am well i wrote a letter to you the 14th in whitch i sent 10 dollars you will probably get it before this one. as to the war news you know more about it as a general thing than i do. i suppose Stonewall Jackson is dead i heard of it right away after the battle some of the prisoners said that he was wounded and then we heard that he was dead. there was not many of the boys that would belive it for some time they said that he had been reported killed to many times to belive it now. one thing is certain he is not bullet proof enny more than other men there was one of our men came back yesterday that was taken prisoner he was the quartermaster Sgt. but we have not heard ennything of the man that is missing from our company. i heard that our general said that our regiment was all dam fools or else they were very brave men at the time we lay in the entrechments under cross fire of the Rebs. at enny rate we done all they asked us to do and when they gave the orders to retreat we done that and in good order and did not make up a very bad face about it eather. i suppose that i could get a furlough to come home in about 3 months if i wanted to but i had rather wait till the married men have been home first. there is one home now and three or 4 have applied for furloughs but they wont let but one out of a company go at a time. as it is getting dark i shall have to stop writeing and i expect to go on guard in the morning   so i will not have enny more time to write so no more this time.

This from your Son
Ira S. Jeffers

May 21st 1863

Dear Sister

I receved your letter today dated the 16th and was glad to hear that you were all well. i am as well as usial and dont have to work very hard at present we are drummed out about daylight then they call the roll then we sweep the streets and then we get our breakfast. then we drill from 7 till half past 8 o'clock then we dont do enny thing more till 4 o'clock and then we have Ballallion drill till six   half past six dress parade whitch finishes up our days work   we have heard from the man that was missing from our company   he was taken prisoner and is now in the paroll camp alive and well. tell Wallace that soldiering aint so bad after you get used to it but the thing of it is to get used to it. i dont think he would like getting used to it   tell him if he thinks he would like it all but the bullets   just to try lying out doors on the ground some rainly night without enny thing only the cloths that he is in the habit of wearing when he is at work   if he can stand that he will do for a soldier and if he cant he wont.

Ira S. Jeffers

Acquia Landing
May 24th 1863

Dear Parents
I recived your letter to day and lose no time in answering it. i am as well as usial and getting fat as a rail.

(William N. Dodge) *He lies like fury for he is getting quite copulant. Hard tack pork coffee sugar are the food that will make a man fat if anything. Well now this is rather imprudent me thinks I hear Ira saying for a fellow to come up and take my pen and paper out of my hand and go to writing, but never mined I wount write any thing bad. Ira is as healthy as one need to be since he had that sick spell before we went upon this last march. And now he looks tough as a bear for the sun has toned him so that in the face he is very near the color of sole leather and to add to his good looks he has had his hair cut or shaved close to his head. But in these respects he resembles all the rest of Uncle Sams boys for this is the style. Well I guess that I will stop now before I spoil his letter entirely. William N. Dodge*

Will has given you discription of my good looks so it will be useless for me to say enny thing. tell grandmother that she need not worry enny thing about me as far as tobaco is concerned for i have about 3 quarters of a pound in my knapsack now. i generly lay in for a supply before my money gets short. i get my paper every week it generly comes a Sunday i got it to day but have not read it yet i though i would write my letter first and i get my envelope and stamp and paper all right every time. and about our provisions on the march we get along as well as could be expected. we carried 8 days rations of hard tack in our knapsack and 3 days rations of pork in our haversacks and then we had beef killed for us the rest of the time but i did not have enny salt and not often that we had fire so the most of the time i eat my beef without cooking or salting. the reds gave us a good shelling one day just for building a fire to cook so after that we went without A fire. i have not enny thing more to write this time so i will let Will finish it.

Ira S. Jeffers

(William N. Dodge) *Well as Ira has left so much paper to go to waste he requested me to write. I will write a few more lines not that I have any thing in particular to write. But as I know that any thing in the shape of a well filed letter even if there is not much sence in it is welcomed. I thought I would fill it up. My self and Ira are sitting at the present moment near where the regt have their washing done. not by a washer woman but a washer man. It is a short distance back from camp. Here we have got away from the noise and confusion of camp. the sun is pouring down hot enough to roast a fellow but get along with it very well so long as they do not set us carrying those Hand Organs as Bob Winner calls the Knapsacks. But after all we do not have it so hard as we might. for my part I never was so healthy in my life. At one time Ira was afraid that he would not stand it very well this summer but at present he is as healthy as any man in the company. Well no more at present. Please tell Uncle Thomsons folks to inquire for a letter at Binghamton for Ophelie from me for I am going to write.*

Yours With respect
Wm N Dodge

Camp near Acquia Landing
June 5th 1863

Dear Sister

I receved a few lines from you yesterday so i thought i must mention your name or you would not write to me as you are receveing letters from other soldiers. i got a letter from Frelia day before yesterday but have not answered it yet nor i shant be in enny hurry to for it had been a long time since i wrote to her and have just receved a answer from it but i had rather have one letter from home than two from enny where else.

I.S.J.

June 6th 1863

Dear Parents

I receved your letter yesterday dated the 30th i did not get time to write till today   yesterday morning we was ordered under arms about day light but we was dissmissed again in a short time   we have got 3 days rations packed ready for another march but we dont know where we are going to march till we get our knapsacks on our backs and get started. there is conciderable sickness in our regiment now   i am well as usial with the exception of a slight cold whitch does not amount to much Will Dodge and Milt are well and so are the rest of the boys in our company that you know. you must tell Wallace that if he dont like to get up so early in the morning nor wate so long for his supper that he must never think of being a soldier. for they would make him get up when they was a mind to and eat when he can get a chance besides haveing to cook his vitels him self that is if he has got enny thing to cook whitch is often. the case that we dont have nothing but Hard Tack whitch is hard enough without enny more cooking and his sleeping arangements he would find would be some different   it is a good school and i think that if he was to come here he would receve a good education that would be remembered by him a long time and he would have a different master from what he has ever had yet. it is not likely that this is very interesting to you or him eather so i will dry up.

This from your Son
Ira S. Jeffers

Camp near Acquia Creek Va.
June 7 1863

Dear Parents

I receved your letter today dated the 25th. i have just come off guard   i have been on guard down on the Ubadan dock for three days.   it is about 2 miles from camp to the dock and about one mile from camp to Acquia Landing. we are not on the same camp ground that we was before the march   we have got just as nice a camp as we had before and in sight of the Potomac it is about a mile from here to that flower garden that i wrote about and i dont get time to leave camp only on Sundays then i most always have letters to write.   the grass has got up so it is good big feed and the apples are as large as Walnuts.   there is not much farming done very near here so i cant tell much how things does look. it is all war around here so folks cant do much farming   we want the most of the ground for camps and drilling grounds. while i was on guard to the dock there was a Steam boat and two barges come in from the South loaded with Contrabands on there way to Washington.   they stopped and left one boat load here and it would be fun for you to have seen them when they landed and met some of there old acquiants who had left about a year ago and hear them inquire about there old Masters and Missus   they are only giving furloughs for 5 days now whitch begins to look as though they intend to make a move again soon.   we cant tell ennything about it but it is not likely that we will lay around a great while   some say that Lee is crossing the Rapahanock. if he is we will likely to have another engagement soon.

Dear Sister

I thought i would write a few lines to you by way of amusement and let you know how much i weigh being you wrote. how much you all weighted you are some heaver than i am for i only weigh 135 lbs. it is so hot here that it takes the fat all off from a fellow i rather think you would look for a shade tree if you was down here. no more at present.

Respectfully yours
Ira S. Jeffers

Camp near Acquia Creek Va.
June 8th 1863

Dear Parents

I receved your letter yesterday dated the 3th and receved one from Uncle George yesterday but i think it will be some time before i answer it for i wrote to him on the 6th of February and he has just answered it. i have not enny letter from Aunt Malina yet and i have writen two letters to her. Catherine said that the corn was up so you could see the rows up north it is larger here where there is enny where they have fed the teams the corn has come up and is about knee high and some of the boys picked ripe Strawberrys more than a week a go. i dont think there is many Strawberrys around here but there is a going to be a good many Blackberrys but they wont last long after they begin to get ripe if we stay here where we are now but we dont know one day where we will be the next. i cant write much news today for it has been such a short time since i wrote before it looked then as if we should have another fight in a few days but i guess we wont unless we are attacked. there is some pieces in the Republican writen by the Ordily Sergeant in our company there was one letter of his in the last paper signed E.L. Wellman and what he writes is calaulated to be true i dont know why there is not more of the Captains letters published i have been expecting to see one of his some time. you must tell Grandmother that she need not worry about raw beef makeing me sick it will not hurt me half as quick as pie and cake would. if i could get a good bowl of johney cake and Milk it would suit me as well as enny thing. i must stop now and go to meeting we have meeting every day between half past one and half past three.

Ira S. Jeffers

Camp near Leesburgh, Va.
June 22th 1863

Dear Parents

I receved your letters yesterday and one from Uncle Lewis. it is the first time we have had enny mail since we started on this march and i have not had enny time or chance to send enny letters and i have not had time to write enny i dont think that we will stay here long we heard heavy fireing yesterday all day and it was so near to us that some of the pickets could hear musketry quite distantly. i dont feel much like writeing for i am quite sleepy for i have been up so much nights and last night i was on picket but i thought i would get a letter ready to send as soon as there was a chance and then sleep afterwards if i could get a chance. my health is good and i have stood the march first rate but there was a good many that had to fall out tell Grandmother that i can get all the cloths that i want as soon as we get into camp and when we are on a march i dont need many. i have got my handkerchief yet and would not take a dollar for it now we have had considerable rain since we started i was out two nights nearly all night when it rained all of the time then had to pitch our tents on the wet ground and lay down with my wet cloths on with out enny fire. you may think that i could not sleep much but i could not help but sleep and did not take cold eather probably Sol can tell you something about marching and laying out in the rain so i will let him talk a spell for me and i will go to sleep. so no more at present i may get a chance to write some more before i send this and i may not.

Ira S. Jeffers

June 22th 1863

Now that i have rested i will write a few more lines   some of the officers have been out beyond the picket lines and came back and said that they had seen a squad of Rebs. the Colnels clerk came round to the companys and wanted 3 men from each company to go and look for the Colnel for he was missing and they have not got back yet. they have been gone about a hour. i do not know enny of the particulars all i know is what i heard the clerk say that he was missing and he wanted 30 men to go and look for him. i will write again as soon as i can   i dont know when i can send this for the mail may go out in the morning and it mat not. P.S. The Colnel has got back all right and so have the boys and i did not see enny rebs eather.

Camp near Edwards Ferry
June 25th 1863

Dear Parents

I thought i would write a few lines to you to let you know that i am well and were i am   we are here now at Edwards Ferry guarding the pontoon bridges. we are in the vicinity of Balls Bluff where Colnel Baker was killed. we dont know how long we shall stay here   the 11th Corps is crossing the river this morning on there way to Harper Ferry   it is not likely that we shall lay here a great while   if you dont hear from me very soon you need not think enny thing strange for when we are on a march i dont get much time to write and if i did get time to write i could not send it. Bob Winner says tell Bill Malkin that it is time for him to come down here now   for the Rebs have crossed the Penn. line again. i think if they are in there they will have a tough time of it before they get out again. i have been about two hours trying to write and i cant think of enny thing so i will stop.

Ira S. Jeffers

Troops protecting pontoon bridge

Camp near Fredrick City
June 28th 1863

Dear Parents

I receved your letter today dated the 23th and lose no time in answering. it is the first time that we have receved enny mail since we left Edwards Ferry and not had enny chance to send enny letters but they say that the mail will go out in the morning at 8 o'clock. i am well and stand the march first rate so far   our rations is prety short just now   some of the boys have not got enny thing for here supper but i have. but i have made out a very good supper and that is about all   the teams will probably be up to us some time tomorrow forenoon. i am in hopes that this move will amount to something. if the Rebs are between us and Pennsylvania there will be likely to be some hard fighting done before they get back acrossed the Potomac again   it is so dark that i cant see to write enny longer tonight but i will write some more in the morning if i can get a chance.

Ira

Dear Parents

As we did not start very early this morning i embrace the opertuity to write a few lines to you to let you know that i am well. we arrived at the battle field near Gettysburg July 1st and was brought into action July 2 between 5 and 6 o'clock and fought till about 9 o'clock. July 3 fighting commenced early in the morning and lasted all day. we was relived two or three times during the day to clean our guns but rest was impossable. July 4th there was not enny fighting where we was to amount to enny thing and we burried our dead. it rained very hard all of the afternoon and nearly all night July 5th. our men went over the brest works this morning and picked up the guns that the Rebs left and burried their dead. got them burried about noon. then we march back to the little town where we are now. i cant tell what is going on now so i will not try for we hear so many romers. Company A and F lost more men than enny of the others. the killed in our company are Horace W. Nicols Malon J. Pardee William W. Wheeler and the acting AGT John VanAmburg who was our ordoly Sargent when we started from Binghamton. the wounded are William N. Dodge Albert Hughs Henery Vanburen James Broadfoot Theodore Spinning and Dannel D. Spinning. the missing are Arron Benn S.W. Matterson Frank Seovil Sammul Seovil Henery J. Vaness George L. Muckey and Joel D. Brown. i can not think of enny more now. the reason why we suffered so much more than the rest of the Regiment was because we was the right of the Regiment and the Rebs flanked us and it was so dark that we could not tell but what they was not our own men for sometime. Will Dodge was doing well the last i heard from him. i heard from him yesterday. he was wounded in the calf of his leg but they say that there was no bones broken. tell Sol that we fought Stonewalls old Brigade and whipped them. the prisoners said that it was the first they had ever been whipped but we had brest works and they did not.

This from your Son
Ira S. Jeffers

Scene behind the breastworks
on Culps Hill, morning of July 3rd

Attack of Johnston's Division
on the breastworks on Culps Hill

P.S. Tell Grandmother that when we get into camp again that i have got something to send her that i picked up on the battle field. i have got a nice Porafolha that i will send to Catherine if i can that i picked up there. tell Sol that the Rebs Act. Agt. General Leigh was killed in front of our brest works July 3 and he lay there when our men went over to bury there dead. our Regimental commission officers that were killed are Captain Gregg   Captain Williams   Lieut. Hallet and Lieut. John H. Vanamburg Act. Agt.

Ira S. Jeffers

This picture taken in November 2007, over 144 years after the battle of Culps Hill still shows visible signs of one of the Confederate burial sites at the base of the mountain.

" Our men went over the breastworks this morning and picked up the guns that the Rebs left and buried their dead. Got them buried about noon"

Ira S. Jeffers
July 6th, 1863

2) On the road towards Sharpsburg
July 9th 1863

Dear Parents

I receved a letter from you yesterday. The mail dont come very often now when we are on the march but when it does i am prety sure to get a letter. we have not been in enny fight since i wrote to you the 6th. My health is good if it was not i could not stand it to march as we are doing. day before yesterday we marched 28 miles and i went on picket after that. But i will try and not grumble nor find fault with the hard marching and the privations that we have to endure for i think it is our duty. i feel confident that peace is close at hand and that i shall soon be home again with my parents and friends. we have 37 men in our company now. Bob winner and Milt knox are both well. Bob has said several times that he was a going to write to Father but he does seem to get at it yet. i saw a SPY yesterday that was hung, he was hanging yet when we came by and they said that he was to hang there three days and he had a son that was to be hung in the afternoon. i guess that i better stop writeing now for i want to clean my Gun. and get things in order while i have a chance. So no more at present.

This From Your Son
Ira

I had got my letter sealded up ready to send but the male came in before i sent it so i broke it open so as to let you know that i receved two letters from you this afternoon. we was in the fight 2 and 3 of July as you will learn by the letter that i wrote you the other day. The 4th we lay in the same position but did not have enny engagement. the loss was heavy on both sides. the loss in our regiment is said to be 143, the place where we fought was near Gettysburg, Pa. we are follering the Rebs as fast as is nessary   we are within 6 miles of Sharpsburg   we halted here. Where we are now about noon and it is nearly dark now and we dont know what moment we may start again. they are said to be entirely sourrounded and the Potomac is up so they cant ford it and our men have distroyed there pontoon bridges so they are in a prety tight spot. the fighting is not done yet but i am in hopes that it soon will be without much more bloodshed. you will hear that Vicksburg is taken probably before you get this.   It is so dark that i cant see to write enny more. you need not send me enny more paper nor envelopes till i write for them but send the stamps the same as you have done.

Ira

Dear Parents

   As i have got a few moments to spare i thought i would write a few lines to let you know that i am well. The regiment lies here in line of battle except companys A and F   they have gone out as skirmishers and i am detailed into the drum corpse for to carry water to the men and to carry the wounded off from the field in case of an engagement. The Musician from our company was wounded at Gettysburg. We crossed Anteitam creek and battle ground yesterday. the rebels dont show much disposition to fight much. the pickets was skirmishing quite sharp a short time ago but every thing is quite now. we are about 3 miles from the Potomac river but i dont know enny name for the place where we are. there is a small town near here and some of the boys say the name of it is Fairplay. i have not heard from Will Dodge since we left Gettysburg. he has gone to Baltamore or Washington probably before this time. he has writen home likely before this time so that you know more about him than i do. the other boys are well i have not much more to write so i may as well stop for this time. Write as often as you can and i will do the same.

Ira

P.S. There is a romer afloat amoung the boys that they are trying to settle this and that the pickets had orders not to fire on one another untill further orders but i dont know how true it is. It may be so and it may not for we hear reports of all kinds.

Ira

2) Pleasant Valley, Maryland
July 16 1863

Dear Parents

We are now in camp for a day or two not far from where we was last fall. my health is good and so are the rest of the boys from our way. i have not heard from Will Dodge since we left him at the hospital   he has written home likely before this time so that you know more about how he is getting along that i do   i have got his letters that have been sent to him since he left the regiment but i cant send them to him yet for i dont know where to direct them. i should think that he would write to me as soon as he could. our Regiment is quite small now i dont know just how many men there is for duty but i think it is two hundred and forty fit for duty. there is a number in the hospitals that will probably be back again before long whitch will be some addition to our number. i cant write much interesting about the march. but if i was with you a spell i could tell you more in one hour than i can write in a week for there has enough transpired for to fill a number of sheets of paper that would be quite interesting to you. it is reported here now that our men have taken Port Hudson and 15000 prisoners and will that make a small hole in the reb army besides it is getting them on a smaller piece of ground that what they have been for a spell back. i suppose that what remaines of Lees army are marching for Richmond as fast as they can. and probably the next letter will be from deep in Va. again.

From your Son
Ira

Dear Parents

I recived your letter today dated the 13th. we have not had enny chances to send letters nor get enny mail since we left Harpers Ferry. we have been marching most of the time since we started from Acquia Creek. we went from Harpers Ferry to Snickers Gap stayed there two days and then to Ashbeys Gap but did not stay there but about two hours and from there to Manassas Gap. we went within about 7 miles of Front Royal. stayed there long enough to get our dinners and then back through Thourofair gap and down by Cattetts Station and Washington Junction. we have had a prety hard time of it and for 3 or 4 days we have been on three quarters day ration now. we have sent some men from our Regiment to escort the conscrips down. i wished it had been so that the soldiers that are here in the field from New York State could have been there to attened the draft. i dont think that they would have made quite so much fuss about it. i cant write much news this time for the mail goes off in about 15 minutes. the boys that are here are all as well as could be expected. Will Dodge is dead. he had his leg amputated before he died. so one of the boys wrote that was in the same hospital. they are calling for the letters.

Ira

Camp near Warrington Junction, Va
July 28th 1863

Dear Parents

I receved a letter from you yesterday and wrote a answer to it but i did not write much for the mail started so soon that i did not have time to write only enough to let you know where i was and how i was getting along. it was the first time that we have had enny mail or chance to send letters since we left Harpers Ferry. when i wrote to you from Littletown i wrote that Will Dodge was wounded in the calf of the leg but no bones broken but i heard afterwards that his leg was broken and last night we had a letter from one of the boys that was in the same hospital that Will was in and he wrote that Will had his leg amputated and died July 13th. he was wounded in the eveing of July 2nd. i dont know whether his folks have heard of it yet or not. i think it is a chance they have. it will be sad news to his folks but tell his mother that he was a brave and good soldier and fell in the defence of his country doing his duty at the head of his company. he was to me almost a brother and now that he is gone it seems almost as though i was left alone amoung strangers. we used to set down and talk of home and friends together and read each others letters. but those times are passed and never to return again. i did not see him after he was wounded. he was taken off to the hospital before i knew that he was wounded. i have got three or four letters that have come to him since he left us and i will wait a spell longer and see if there is enny more comes here to him and then i will take them to the Chaplin and have him send them home to his folks.

From your Son
Ira

Dear Parents

As it has been some time since i have writen i will try and write a long letter for it may be some time before you will hear from me again and you may hear from me quite often if we stay in this vicinity. we will be likely to have a chance to send letters every day. Captain Shipman has gone to the hospital. he went since we stopped here and it is the opinion of some that he will not come back again. Milt Knox and Luke Cresson are both well and Bob Winner is well but when we are on a march i think i can stand more that he can. you wrote that you though that the fighting was about done on the Potomac for this time but i do not think so. i think that the engagement has become general all through the Confederated States and it will be kept up all summer and that they will keep us agoing as long as we can stand it and then they will go into camp a day or two long enough to wash up a little and drew clothing and if they do and things are conducted as they should be i think that this summer will close the war. the Army of the Potomac is doing some big marching this summer. we have marched 20 miles in a day a good many times and one day we marched 28 miles that i know of and i think we have done it more that once. you can make some calculation about what kind of times we have marching. for some days back we have had reville at half past two and marched at 4 and marched all day and stopped about dark then we had to get water and wood and build our fires and cook our supper and drew rations and then put up our tents. or go with out them and by the time we get to bed we have to sleep fast or else we dont sleep much. but i wont grumble or make enny fuss as long as there is enny prospects of bringing this to a close.

Ira.

I think that as i have plenty of time that i might as well keep on skribbing. Captain Eldrige is here all right. you wanted to know how i get along for money. i get along first rate. i have not had but one cent since we left Acquia Creek and i dont know as i want enny. if we should go into camp for about two weeks i think we would get our pay but it dont look much like we are staying here for i have seen three trains go by today loaded with pontoons boats. they will probably put a bridge acrossed the Rapahaneck tonight or tomorrow. i think that we are going to Gordonsville but i dont know whether we are or not. there was another train just gone by loaded with pontoon boats. i shall have to stop writing now for we are going to have inspection in about 5 minutes. i may get a chance afterwards to write a few lines but i guess i have wrote about enough for this time so i will get my letter finished so as to get it in the office in time. i dont know what kind of weather you have up north but it is as plenty warm enough here for comfort and a little warmer. i forgot to say that i got my paper yesterday.

Ira

Camp near Warrinton Junction, Va.
July 30 1863

Dear Parents
I receved two letters from you yesterday mailed the 24th and 27th and also my paper of the 22th and whitch had the list of drafted men in Broome County. i think that Father has got rather the wrong idea about the drafted men not haveing to leave the north or see enny fighting for we have sent men from this regiment as well as from others to conduct them down here as soon as possable. but i think that if the men that are drafted can stand as much as we can of the marching and the victorys that we have gained. are taken the advantage of that this war will soon be brought to a close i think it will be prety hard for the boys to come down here now at this season of the year to commence marching although i dont think that the weather is much warmer here than it is in New York State. at enny rate the rebs said that they had a hotter time of it in Pennsylvaina that they ever see in Virginia tell Sol that i would like to have him write a letter to me first rate and if he has to come down here to try and come in this regiment. there is a good many boys here that he is acquainted with but i dont much expect to see him come on this draft. some of the boys are hightly pleased to see the names of some that are on the list of drafted. i want father to take darn good care of his young horse and that i have got another watch that i dont know but i shall send home to him prety soon if i dont get it cleaned. it is a Hunter case Cilinder Escapement. Warrented to be a good time piece valued at 15 dollars but it did not cost me the half of 15 out of pocket. i found a revolver and i gave that and to give 5 dollars next pay day the revolver i did not want and i

did not want to carry it so i managed to get it into a compass and i think that i have got good pay for the revolver.

Ira S. Jeffers

Camp near Kempers Ford
August 2nd 1863

Dear Parents

I have a chance to write to you again   we are now at Kempers Ford on the Rapahanock River   we got here yesterday and our regiment was left here to guard this Ford. we was fixing our camp yesterday so i did not get a chance to write till today   our camp is about half a mile from the river. the Rebs are on the other side of the river in sight of our pickets and one of them swam acrossed yesterday and made our boys a visit   we have got some old breastworks that we are fixing up besides some new ones that we are building. i dont think that they have got enny force here only just enough for pickets. it brings us on duty prety often just now for we have a good many for pickets and quite a large detail for to work on the breastworks   i was on picket night before last and on guard last night but i think after we get the breastworks done that we will have some chance to rest. we heard cannonading yesterday nearly all day and as near as i could learn it was between Culpper and Raphanock Station and the news was that our men drove the Rebs and took 15 hundred prisoners but i dont know how true it is. when you write again you may send paper and envelopes the same as you did before and you may send me two dollars but dont send enny more   i rather you would not send but one dollar than send more than two. i have got Wills letters ready to put in the office to send to his folks   i have written a letter to Uncle Lew and one to Aunt Malvina   i wrote them when i was at Warrington Junction   i have got a piece of the rebel Adg. Gen. Leights coat that was killed. you will find enclosed that i send to Catherine as a momento of the battle of Gettysburg i have got a pair of shears that i picked up on the battlefield that i would like to send to Grandmother if i could but i cant send them by mail. i will not write enny more now but i will often when i aford the time.

Ira

Camp near Kempers Ford
August 7th 1863

Dear Parents

I have just receved a letter from you dated the 2nd and lose no time in answering it   my health is good with the exception of a dierea that i have had for a few days but it is better now. the boys are all enjoying prety good health at present   we have got a nice place for a camp it is in the edge of the woods so that we can lie in the shade when we are off from duty   it is prety warm weather here   you must tell Grandmother that she must not worry about my being sick for if i am sick i shall write and let you know. yesterday was the day that the President set apart for Thanksgiving and prayer and we held our services here in the woods and it was attended by all of the soldiers in camp. we have a good Chaplin and i like his speaking very much   the Chaplin told us yesterday that one more of the great leaders of the rebellion was dead   you will probably remember seeing his name was Yancy. i think now that the war is prety near at a end   we may see some more fighting but i am in hopes that it will be settled with out enny more blood shed   but i want to have it settled right for i think there has been to many lives lost for the old flag not to have it settled enny other way but right. you said that you heard that Colnel Ireland had gone to Elmira to get drafted men to fill up his regiment he did not go but he had sent men   they started nearly two weeks ago. our Corps is guarding the river   they are strung all along. a regiment is guarding this place in place of our regiment at this ford   it is a small one and we have got a prety good position   the rebel cavelry pickets are in sight on the other side but they aint got much force there   i dont think there is more than 50 of them   just enough to watch our movements to see that we dont attempt to cross. we taken two or three prisoners since we have been here but they wanted to get out of the war. i saw in the paper the other day that Lousanannia was ready to come back in the Union and that North Carolina was ready to follow her and two of the boys that we took the other day was from Lousanannia and they said that the boys from that state was deserting as fast as they could. the Leut. has just got a letter from some of the boys that was taken prisoner but i have not heard it read yet. i have got my sheet about full so i must stop. send me two or three good pens.

Ira S. Jeffers

August 11th 1863

Dear Parents

I receved your letters dated the 5th day before yesterday but I was on picket duty and could not get A pen to write with till today. I am on picket yet but we are to be relived tonight there aint much going on here we dont have much to do only picket duty. it is prety hot weather here it is so hot that our shirts are wet through even if we set in the shade but the nights are cool so that we sleep first rate. our rations have been prety short since we got into camp for we had got ahead of them while we was on the march but we have got catched up now so that we draw our full rations. apples are getting about ripe so we have lived on apple sauce when we did draw meat enough we would try and find A Beef or A Sheep or something of that sort. it is prety hard work to starve the soldiers as long as there is cattle A running around the corn is getting large to pick now and I think that will suffer some. we dont see many Rebs here now I saw two this morning on the other side of the river rideing around but I dont think that there is many near here. if there is they lie in the shade the most of the time as well as our men I expect that we shall get our pay in A few days they say the Paymaster is on his way here now. our boys have been fixing up the camp all day they are going to have inspection this afternoon by General Geary. then I suppose that if everything is in order that they will get furloughted. I saw in the paper that Meads army was to have furloughts allowing them to be gone from 20 to 30 days so they will have time to make quite A visit. they aint many men in the company now but it will be some time before they get around so that they all can go home. I will not write enny more now for I cant send my letter till morning then I may have something more to write. P.S. you wanted to know if I had heard any thing from Osker Knowlan. nothing only what you have wrote whitch is enough   you will laugh when you see how I have spelled his name but I did not think how to spell it at first.

Ira S. Jeffers

Camp near Kempers Ford
August 12th 1863

Dear Parents

We did not get relived from picket till this morning so I did not get into camp in time enough to send my letter. so I thought that I would have it ready to send in the morning. I got A letter from Uncle Lew today we expect to get our pay tomorrow. the paymaster is in the brigade and they said that he would be ready to pay us tomorrow and as soon as I get my pay I will send you the check whitch will probably be 40 dollars and the rest of the money I guess I shall keep this time for I am oweing about six dollars of it. that will leave me six dollars for spending money. I dont know but what I shall sell my watch if I do shant want to keep much and if I keep my watch I shall have to get it cleaned and A crystal put in it. it costs so much to get it fixed that I hate to be put to the expence of fixing it if I could get A chance to I would send it home and let Father keep it for me.

Ira S. Jeffers

Dear Parents

I receved A letter from you today dated the 9th and was glad to hear that you was all well. I am sorry to hear of the reports that you tell about. the letters that came to Will after the battle of Gettysburg the Captain took and opened except one whitch I had take the envelope off from before I could get them into another envelope but I did not read them nor enny body else. the Captain opened them in my presence to see if there was money in them so if I should lose the letters that I would not lose the money but there was no money in them. one of them had 12 stamps whitch were stuck together and the Captain said that he would take them and use what of them that was good. I supposed that he intended to pay Mr. Dodge for the stamps but that was nothing to me   I took the letters and sent them to his folks because I thought it was my duty to and I thought it would be there wish. as it is I am sorry that I had enny thing to do with the letters at all. as to the Captain he was in the battle. he was with us the night the Rebs flanked us. where we lost the most of our men and he was with us the next day till we got relived from the entrenchments. the next day when we was burying the dead he took charge of the men that was detailed to bury them. I think that of those that are at home reporting such romers would come down here and do as much as Captain Shipman has done that it would be far better. I have got my money all right and am much obliged to him for sending it to me. I receved Sols letter this morning and shall try and answer it soon. I have spent one dollar of my money already I have brought me a gold and a silver holder. I had got tired of borrowing and waiting for others to get through writing before I could write.

Ira

P.S. August 14th. We got our pay today and you will find inclosed A check of 40 dollars. I dont know as I have got enny news to write today so no more this time.

From your son
Ira S. Jeffers

Camp Near Kempers Ford, Va.
August 16th 1863

Dear Parents

I recived your letter last night dated August 12th and was glad to hear that you was all well. I wrote A letter to you the 14th and sent you my check of 40 dollars and as soon as you get it write and let me know that it has come safe. the weather is some cooler now then what it has been and the nights are quite cool. you need not be surprised if you dont get A letter from me again in some time. we have got marching orders but I dont think we shall march very soon. If we stay I shall write often. I have not much to write this morning for it has been so short A time since I wrote. I am well and so are the rest of the boys that you know except Bob Winner. he has got another spell of the ear ache otherwise we are injoying ourselves first rate eating apples an green corn we dont see many cucumbers that you tell about. but you must save some for pickles so that you can send me some next Winter. I wrote to you about the captain the other day and you will probable get that letter before you do this one. I have not heard enny thing about the captains being courtmarsheled nor about his resigning. I cant write about enny thing that I dont know enny thing about. Ask father if he dont know hank Shipman yet. I would not be surprised if the captain was not well enough to come back. but I dont think that he has been courtmarsheled.

Afternoon August 16th

We are expecting to march in the morning. they say that the first Divison of our corps has already gone. And as near as I can learn we are going back to our old camp at Acquia Creek.

Ira Jeffers

Tell Polly that I was surprised to recive A letter from her and to see what A good writer she was and Catherine had better look out as Polly will soon get so that she can beat her at writing.

Ira Jeffers

Camp near Kempers Ford
August 23th 1863

Dear Parents

I receved three letters last night. two from you and one from Aunt Malvina   and was glad to hear that you was all well   my health is prety good. I have got the head ache some this afternoon   I commenced to write this morning but I had not writen about two lines before I was called on to take a man up to the Division Headquarters to be put in the Provost guard for disobedience to his officers. It was about five miles up there and back again and it is A very warm day so that I feel prety tired for I was not gone over two hours but I thought that I must answer your letters today. I expect to have to go out on picket tomorrow then I shall be out three days but I can come into camp to send letters and get them if I want to. the Rebs are in sight on the other side of the river yet but we dont fire on one another pickets   one of the Rebs come down to the river the other day and wanted to know if the same Brigade lay here now that did when when he was taken prisoner and the boys told him no. he said yes they did to for he was over here where we was A camping the other night and was within 10 paces of us. that was what some of the boys said that was down there   we had taken him prisoner once and he got away and if he gets taken again he will probably be hung for A spy. his wife and sister live between our camp and the river   we are all looking for the fall of Charleston with anxious eyes   I think Old Lee will have to fall back to Richmond then   I think that when Charleston is taken the war will be about done. I saw in the papers that the 89th has gone down there. tell Kate that I wrote A letter to her the other day that took up two sheets of paper but after I got it sealed up that I found out that I had not enny stamps to put on it so I put it in my partfafolia and forgot it so that I will send it this time. I will wait till I get time to write her another letter.

Ira S. Jeffers

1) Camp near Kempers Ford Va.
August 31th 1863

Dear Parents

I recived your letter last night of the 27th and was glad
to hear that you was all well. I am well and am on picket   I
have been on picket A week today. Wilt and Bob are both
out here too and we are employing ourselfs first rate. I wrote
one letter to Aunt Malvina since I have been out here and
have commenced two different times to answer Sols letter
and have not answered it yet. I shall try and write to Emiline
and Grandfather Scofield today. if he prises my letters so
highly I will try and write to him oftener. we aint got enny
Captain. Leiutnant Corbitt has command of the company
while the Captain is gone and Leiutnant Sage has command
of company G at preasant   so we have not got many officers
now. Wilt is A good Corporal and gets along well. he says
that he has so many letters to write that he can not write to
all that he would like to but he says that he will try and write
to Father as soon as he can. he commenced to write to him
once but did not have time to finish it and you know that
he must write to his folks before enny body else. I have got
my diary yet but it is prety well worn   it looks as though it
had seen some hard service. I get my paper every week and
Milt gets the Democrat and Bob gets A paper from Sullavan
County every week. I want to know if you have got that
likeness yet that I had taken for you yet and do you think
as much of it as you would of me taken with the uniform
on. I dont know but what I shall have one taken prety soon
to send to Catherine then you can see how I look now. I
dont see as I look enny different from what I did when I
enlisted all though I am one year older than I was then but

I aint enny bigger. Bob has just come back from camp   he says tell you that he is well and will write as soon as he can find enny thing to write about. I have just wrote A letter to Grandfather and have got it ready to send with this one. no more this time.

Ira S. Jeffers

1) Camp near Kempers Ford Va.

Sept 2 1863

Dear Sister

I recived your letter of the 30th today and as it is not quite dark yet I thought that I would commence my letter tonight. I have just been up to the Davison Head Quarters and had my likeness taken whitch I am going to send to you. I did not put my equipment on for I though that it would look better without them but if you had rather have one with them on next pay day I will have another taken just as you want it. the star that is on my coat belongs on our caps. it is to show what Corps. and what division we belong to. the red star is the first division of the 12th Corps. the white star is the 2nd and the blue is the 3rd division. there is no other Corps. that has the star. we have not got but two divisions in our Corps. now. Mother wanted that I should write the number of the division and General so I may as well write the whole. it is the 3rd Brigade and Brig. General Green 2nd Division General Geary   12th Corps. Major General Slocum.

September 3th

Dear Sister

I am going on camp guard this morning but I will have time to finish my letter for it will not go out till tomorrow morning. we have not had enny conscrips yet   there was some sent up to the 111th Regt. last night   they are right in sight of our Regt. I have not been over to see them yet but some of our boys have and they say that they dont feel as good as the old soldiers do but they will get used to our fair after A while. now as I have got on guard and I shant come on in two hours so I can finish my letter   I will send you the likeness in this letter and I want that you should write as soon as you get it and let me know if it got through safe. I should be sorry to lose it   it cost me one dollar but I would not have it lost for that price.

From Ira S. Jeffers
to His Sister

1) Camp near Kempers Ford Va.
Sept 6th 1863

Dear Sister

It has been but A few days since I wrote you but I though that I would commence A letter and finish it by the time that I get off from Picket. I am on picket now at the Ford. the Rebs have got A picket post on the other side of the river oppisite of us and our posts aint farther than from the house down to the railroad. and the river is quite narrow here the Rebs came down to the river his morning with A flag of truce and wanted to send A woman and A couple of children acrossed on to this side of the river. she was on that side of the river on visit when we came here and could not get back till we was A mind to let her. we sent A man acrossed to help her over. they crossed on the dam and A few minutes ago there was two of the Johneys come down to the side of the river and set down there A spell but we are not allowed to talk with them now.

Sept 7th

Dear Sister

I am setting down on the bank of the river writeing and the Rebs are setting on the other side watching us but I dont care how long they set there as long as they behave themselfs. it looks hard to see us here so close together mortal enemys to one another and dont know what minute the other will fire on them. it would be quite A sight for some of the boys up north to see A wild Reb loose A running around in the woods just as they are A mind to and I shant be very sorry to see them when they get tame so that they wont bite. I wrote A letter to you the other day and sent my likeness to you and now I want that you should all have yours taken and send to me if you can have them taken on paistboard or cards for I can carry them in my portoflia and when you write again I like to have you send me about 12 stamps.

This from your affectanate
Brother Ira.

Sept 9th

Dear Sister

I will finish my letter so it will go in the mail this morning. I came off from picket yesterday but the mail had gone out and wont go out again till morning. I have not got enny news to write only that Captain Shipman got back last night. I have not had A chance to say enny thing to him yet. he looks as though he was A good deal better than when he went away. he has got his whiskers shaved off so that he looks different from what he did when he went away. I have not got much time to write for the mail will go out in A few minutes so no more at present.

Ira S. Jeffers

Mail wagon leaving Headquarter
Post Office, Army of The Potomac

Camp near Kempers Ford Va.
Sept 12th 1863

Dear Sister

I receved your letter last night of the 8th and was glad
to hear from you again   it has been some time since I have
had A letter from home. I am well and am on picket but I
have just as good A chance to write as though I was in camp
tell Sol that I have commenced twice to write to him once
I waited for Bob to write   he said he would write some in
it. after I had got through he and I waited so long for him
that I would not send it but I will write to him as soon as I
get some stamps. I wrote for some in the last letter. I was
pleased to hear that you receved my likeness all right and that
you think that it is A good one but I dont think that I am
very fat but I know that I dont look as poor as I did when we
came here. the Captain says that we are all as fat as pigs now
but he says when he went away that our faces was as long as
A rail. and I think that we had cause to look so sad we had
had A long and servier march and some of the time we did
not have but three quarters rations. but it dont take but A
short time to get rested up again. when we get into camp
the government furnishes enough when we are where that it
can be got to us. I would like to have had my likeness taken
when we came out of the fight at Gettysburg for I had not
washed me in three days and fro twenty four hours I did not
eat A mouthful of enny thing. I guess that if you could have
seen us then you would have though that we looked poor
enough and black enough but every thing must have an end
and so did the fight at Gettysburg but I though that it was A
long time comming. there was some of the letters that I sent
to you that I did not direct so I am not quite as good A writer

as you though I was. it will be A long time I think before I get so that I can write as good as that was writen. tell Albert that if he can get as much for his tobacco as I have to pay for mine that he will soon be A rich man but I dont think that he can. write as often as you can and I will try and do the same   it dont cost much to write only the stamps and if you will send me stamps enough I will write as often as twice A week while we are in camp.

This from your brother
Ira S. Jeffers

Camp near Kempers Ford Va.
Sept 13th 1863

Dear Parents

I wrote A letter to Catherine yesterday but I though that I would write again today for I dont know but what we shall have to march soon   so I though that if I did not get A chance to write you would know what the reason was there is considerable cannonading going on up the river this morning and the Leiutant Colnel has just been down here and told us to have our things packed up so as to be ready to march at A moments notice. we may start before tomorrow morning and we may not move from here in some time yet. it is uncertian one day what we will be doing the next I dont think that the fireing that I hear will amount to much but I cant tell but what it will be A big fight yet. it is probably our caverlry makeing a reconnosence acrossed the river at Kelleys Ford. I am on picket today and shall be relived in the morning and guess that if we dont move that I will not finish my letter till I get back to camp. the fireing seems to be further off than it was A short time ago   I have got my diary yet and have just been writing some in it.

This from your Son
Ira S. Jeffers

1) Camp near Kempers Ford Va.
Sept 14th 1863

Dear Parents

We was relived from pickets this morning the weather is getting prety cool now and we begin to have cold rains but I like the cold weather better than I do the hot weather. the report in camp today is that our forces made A reciniusence acrossed the river yesterday and that our men drove them acrossed the Rapadan river. there pickets have left the river in front of us. they left yesterday about 4 o'clock so there is none to be seen this morning. some think that the Rebs are going to fall back to Richmond but I dont know what they intend to do Mother you must not think that because I have writen to Catherine that I entended to slight you I want that you should write as often as you can and now that Catherine has got time so she can write I shall look for letters quite often. I dont know why it is but I think A great deal more of A letter from you than from enny body else and tell Father that I want that he should try and write to me and write what he thinks about the war news he has not writen enny in some time and if he is waiting for me to write to him first please write and let me know. but I suppose that his hands are stiff to write much.

This from your Son
Ira S. Jeffers

1) Camp near Raccon Ford Va.
on the Rapadan River
September 18 1863

Dear Parents

We got here yesterday about 10 o'clock and went into camp but I dont know how long we shall stay. we was paid off again today   we got two months pay and I will send you the check of twenty dollars in this letter. this afternoon we was all brought up into line to see two men shot that had deserted. it is A sad sight to see fellow men shot in that way but there must be A stop to Deserting some way and A man knows before he deserts what the sentence is for such an offence   I have not got A great deal of time to write now for the mail will go out at five o'clock. I am well as usial except having the tooth ache A little   the other boys from our way are all well. I wrote for some stamps some time ago but I have not got them yet   I expect them now every day   I had to borrow one to put on this letter. I shall have to finish my letter right away for the mail will go out soon and I want to be sure to get it in in time. so no more this time   next time I will try and write A longer letter.

Ira S. Jeffers

Camp near Racoon Ford Va.
Sept 20th 1863

Dear Parents

I receved your letter the eveing of the 18th but did not have time to answer it till today and it is not very comforable writing today for it is so windy and setting in one of these tents is not much protection from the wind. I receved the stamps all right we got our pay the 18th and I wrote A letter the same day and sent the check of twenty dollars. the weather is prety cold here now and we are having some cold rains. I think likely that it is as cold here now as it is up north I though last night that we would have to fight all night but as it turned out we did not. about A hour before sundown we heard sharp musket fireing and we was ordered into line immeditatly but news soon came to our relive that it was our cavelry that had been out on A scout that was dischargeing their pieces. I would be quite A sight for you if you could have seen us we are in A lot of about 50 acres and it is completly covered with tents and wagons and artillery. all most every thing that belongs to an army there was two deserters shot here last Friday it looked hard but the Milatary law is very strict in such cases and it will probably be A warning to those that witnessed it. I hope that I shall never be temped to desert Captain Shipman is well and is as fat as ever. Mr. Bacon has been sick for some time but he has been so as to be in the company   when we started on this march he was sent to the Invalid Corps but his papers was not made out right so he was sent back   he will probably be sent again in A few days   he has got A very sore sore on his shoulder but it is getting better now. he has been A good soldier but he cannot stand it in the field enny longer   he should have been sent away before. now he has got 5 boys in the service I think. Bob Winner is well and so is Milt Knox and Luke Cresson   I am well except that I have had the tooth ache lately   I got cold in my face but they dont trouble me much now. I will not write enny more this time but I will try and write as often as I can.

This from your Son
Ira

Camp near Racoon Ford Va.
Sept 24 1863

Dear Sister

I receved your letter last night with Grandfathers likeness and the stamps. I think the likeness is A good one so do the other boys tell Grandmother to send me hers as soon as she can. I cant write much this time for we have got orders to march and our things are all packed up and I expect to hear the orders to fall in every minute. I am well the Chaplain is calling for the letters now so no more this time.

Ira S. Jeffers

On the march
Sept 25 1863

Dear Parents

I receved your letter this morning and as we have not started yet I thought that I would try and write A few lines to you to let you know that we are on the move we are near the railroad now and they are turning in the teams and say that we are going by rail this time. we have got 8 days rations and are bound for some place some say that we are going to Tennessee and some say North or South Carolina. it is quite certain that we are going some distance. I have not got A very poor place to write and am in something of a hurry for I dont know how soon we shall start. I wrote A few lines to Catherine yesterday before we started from camp I will write to you as often as I can but I may not have A chance to write again very soon and if I do I may not be where I can send it. the bugle is sounding now so no more for now.

Ira

Sept 27 1863

I did not have a chance to send my letter till today and I had not sealed it up so I though that I would try and slip this in it. we are at Realton station now and expect to take cars tonight. the First Division has gone. I expect that we shall go to Tennessee to reniforce Rosecrance so it is not likely that I shall have A chance to write again very soon and if I do I may be where I cannot send it.

Ira

Bellair, Ohio
Oct 1st 1863

Dear Parents

As I have A chance to write A few lines I thought that I would try to let you know where I am now we have just got off from the cars and crossed the Ohio River at Bellair about 5 miles below Wheeling. it is the first time we have been off from the cars since we started from Realton Station. I expect that we are going to Tennessee under our old Commander General Hooker. it is so cold that I can hardly write it is only A few minutes after sunrise now the boys all enjoy themselfs first rate. it is some easier than carrying Knapsacks all of the time but it is hard enough to ride in the cars all of the time. we dont get much sleep it is pretty cool but we are going in A swimming now so more this time. I will write as soon as I can.

Ira

Nashville, Tennessee
Oct 6 1863

Dear Parents

I have not had A chance to write to you in some time so I will try and write A few lines   we have just got here to Nashville and have got off from the cars and are lying around the Depot. I dont know yet where we are A going to. the Rebs have burnt A bridge about 30 miles from here and probably that is the reason why we have stoped here. I have heard that the Corps Head Quarters is at Murfresborough and I think very likely that it is for the present.

Oct 6th

I had to stop writing for we had to fall in and pitch our tents for the night   it is raining quite hard now and it is so cold that I can hardly write. our Regiment is the only one that is left here   the rest have gone to Murfresborought   some think that we are to stay here but I think that we are left to guard A wagon train but they are apt to be right as I am   we will be likely to know tomorrow   we have had A prety good ride on the cars   we have been through the District of Columbia and states of Maryland, Western Virginia   Ohio   Indiana Kentucky and as far as Nashville in Tennessee and I dont know how much farther we have got to go but I guess that we shall come to A halt before long.

Oct 7th

I will try and finish my letter this morning. I dont know what we are going to do yet but it is likely that the officers do by this time   I have not had A letter since we left Virginia for the mail has not been sent to us. we will get it probably before long   I cannnot write much more this time for I have got to clean up my gun and other traps. so as to be ready for enny duty that they may want me for. so no more at presant.

From your Son
Ira

Fosterville, Tenn.
Oct 17th 1863

Dear Parents

I receved your letter yesterday dated the 2nd of Oct and one from Catherine that she wrote at Whitneys Point and one from Afredia and my paper of the 7th and I got my paper today of the 14th. I wrote A letter to you when I was at Nashville and one when we was at Tullahoma we went as far as Dechert Station with the wagon train then we marched back as far as Wartrace. that is where Slocums headquarters is then we took the cars to this place whitch is but A few miles from Murfriesburough we are guarding the railroad here. we had A prety rough time when we was guarding the train for it rained every day but one all of the time that we was with it   we got here night before last and worked all day yesterday and part of the day today but it is raining quite hard now. we built board tents so that it is quite comfortable if they will let us stay A spell and enjoy them we will be satisfied but there is A rumer in camp now that our Corps is going to the front in A few days. if we stay here A spell till I get straighten around so that I can I will try and write you A good long letter. I saw General Grant day before yesterday when he went through on the cars they say that he is going to take the place of General Rosencrance but I dont know how that is. Bob Winner is well but I am not very well nor very sick I have had the Dirarie for A couple of days but I am better now. I am not so but what I can eat my rations I will get all of the letters that you have sent just the same that as directed to Washington but I dont think I will get them quite as soon as I will to have them directed to Nashville. you may direct to Company "F" 137 Regt. NYSV, 12th Corps, Nashville, Tenn. if they keep us moveing around so much I cannot write very often but I want that you should write as often as twice A week enny how for I shall get them after A while and an old letter is new to me. and I will write as often as I can.

This from your Son
Ira

Tullahoma, Tenn.
Oct 23, 1863

Dear Parents

We started from Nashville the 12th with A wagon train for the 11th Corps. our Corps is strung all along the railroad from Nashville to this place and our Brigade is at Murfriesburough and after we get through with this train we expect to go back to Nashville or to Murfriesburough. some of the officers think that our Corps will guard the railroad this winter if we do I think that we will have a prety good time I receved two letters from you when we got to Murfriesburough dated the 21 and 27th of September so it seems that you have not heard that we had started for Tennessee when you wrote. it is not likely that we will get enny more letters till we get back to the Brigade then I will try and write oftener that what I have for A spell back. we have been moveing around so much that I have not had much time to write. tell Catherine that I have been to Shelbeyville where Uncle Tom was owned by Mister Shelbey the Old Man is dead but the young man that went down south too but Uncle Tom is back living yet but he is an old man now. I mean the Uncle Tom that we used to read about in "Uncle Toms Cabin". I did not see Shelbey but the inhabitants told us about it and when we came through Alexandra Va. I saw Pete Jay he was to work there in the machine shop on the railroad. he looked as tough and fat as A Bear and I dont think that I am very poor for I was weighted when we was at Shelbeyville and weighted 142 pounds. tell Grandfather that Hiram Bulock is here with us he is in our Company but the other boys that you wrote about I dont know enny thing about. it is so windy that I cant write very well for I have not got enny tent up so I will not write enny more this time.

This from your Son
Ira

Direct to Nashville, Tenn.
Direct To Ira S. Jeffers   Company "F"   137th Regt. N.Y.S.V.
3rd Brigade, 2nd Division, 12th Corps Nashville, Tenn.

1) Near the Battle Field of Wauhatehie
November 1, 1863

Dear Parents

It has been some time since I have had A chance to write to you but it has not been because I have not wanted to I wrote to you when we was at Fosterville the day before we started from there   we took the cars at Fosterville one week ago today and came as far as the cars would run for the bridge is burnt acrossed the Tennessee River and the Rebels held the way to Chattanooga but we have marched down the railroad till we got here at the foot of Lookout Mountain. we got here the 28th and that night about 12 o'clock we was attacked and had quite a sevier fight. it lasted about two hours then the Rebs had to draw back and hunt for there holes in Lookout Mountain again   there was but A small force of us engaged but there was to many of us for the Rebs. our Regiment suffered badly   there was 15 killed 75 wounded and 5 missing. the loss in our Company was 2 killed and 11 wounded some of whitch has died since they went to the hospital. Hiram Bullock was wounded in the thigh and Egder Elwell wounded in the thigh.   Luke Cresson was wounded and I have heard that he has died since he went to the hospital   I dont think of enny others that you would know at present. we fought the same men that we did at Gettysburg and Chanslorville   we are haveing a prety hard time of it here now   we have moved back A short distance from the place where we had the fight and have went to building entrenchments   we are up night and day but I will not grumble about the hardships. sometimes I get discouraged A little and say things that I dont mean to but I try and do my duty without enny murmers. Bob winner

is well and he is Corporal Robert H. Winner now   Milt is
well. there is fireing occasionally from Lookout Mountain
but they are not throwing their shells in this direction. if
the Rebs dont Evacuate the mountain there will probably be
A heavy fight soon. I am on Head Quarters guard today so
that I have had A chance to write A letter and would like to
write more if I had time. no more at present.

This from your Son
Ira S. Jeffers

P.S. General Green was wounded in the mouth

Near Lookout Mountain, Tenn
Nov 4th 1863

Dear Parents

I wrote A letter to you the 1st of this month but as I have time I thought that I would write A few lines to you today   I wrote that we had been in A fight and you will probably get that letter before you do this one. so there is no use of my writing about it again   we have moved back A short distance from where the fight was and have built up breast works and have got them nearly finished now. I have not heard from the boys that went to the hospital but once   Luke Cresson died after he went to the hospital   Hiram Bullock was wounded in the thigh but I heard that was no bone broken   Edger Elwell was wounded in the thigh slighty. I will try and give you the names of all the wounded in the Company. killed G.W. Doolittle and H.E. Bayles wounded Hiram Bullock   Edger Elwell   Senica Williams   Colba Wales   James A. Ainsworth Elizah Hawkins   Newton Hunt   George W. Kilburn   Eugene Martin and W.D. Mattoon.   James D. Cresson died since this I think is A correct list from our Company. the number of men now with the Company is 25. the Regiment is only about twice as large as our Company was when we came out. there is quite A number in the hospitals that I suppose will be back to the Regiment some time or other. the prisoners that we took are sick of the war and wish that it would end they say that they are satisfied that they cant whip us   I think when this war is ended that there will never be another Secession in the United States.

November 7th 1863
I did not have time to finish my letter the other day and the next day I went on picket and was out two days and when I

got into camp today I was so busy that I did not have time to write till tonight. I receved A letter from you today dated the 24th and mailed the 26th and I got my paper today I get my paper as regular as I could expect. we dont get our mail very regular sometimes we get it once A week and sometimes twice or three times but it comes very acceptable enny time and old letters are new to us and are well read.

Eveing November 7th 1863

Dear Parents

I wish that you could look into our tents just now and see what we are doing away down here in Tennessee. there is Milt Knox and John Hanley and myself all of us writing we have got A candle so that we have A good light and we are trying to make good use of it   I mean to write as often as I can and if you dont get letters very often you must not wate long before you write for I look for A letter every time we get A mail Father wanted that I should write about all of the boys and I have writen about all of them in our Company I think that you know   there is some in other companys that you know that I did not mention. our Leiutenat Colnel was wounded and our Birgadier General was wounded and our Colnel has command of the Brigade. and Leiutenat Corbett that was in the company was wounded and John Dorman that used to work for Grandfather Scofield was wounded and John Thompson was wounded. I dont think of enny more now of the wounded that you would know   it was but A small fight but it was just as bad for our Regiment as though there had been more troops engaged. but I think that I shall remember my 20th Birthday for some time. but I did not get A licking to remember it by. there was about two hundred of the Rebels came in and gave themselfs up today and I wish it had been two thousand. the Captain is well and they keep him prety busy now A days   they do not send him on picket nor put him on much of enny milatary duty. they send him out with fatigue partys to build roads and to chop down the timber that is in the way. he is the best man in the Regiment for that and if he could soldier it in that way all of the time he would it like first rate but the marching is to much for him   he is to old and fleshy tomorrow is Sunday and then we are to have inspection so what I write will have to be done tonight and I think that I have writen A good long letter for one eveing even if there is not much interesting in it and I will try and write again soon. the Rebel Brigade officer of the day came into our lines and gave himself up today so our Leiutenat has just told us. the more that gives up the better it suits us. some of the Rebs that came in told our Boys that they thought that the war would end in less than 60 days for they said that just as soon as there was A big fight that they would desert. but that is there word for it   it may be so.

This from your Son
Ira S. Jeffers

Camp near Lookout Mountain Tenn
Nov 12th 1863

Dear Sister

It has been sometime since I have writen A letter to you so I thought that I would try and write A few lines to you this eveing. I do not get many letters now and I should think that you folks at home could find time to write quite often I write as often as I can I receved A letter from you and Father and Mother the 7th and answered it that eveing. I expect to go out on picket in the morning and be out three days we are camped in the same place that we was when I wrote to you before and we are building log tents. it is the talk now that we shall stay here the rest of the winter unless something new turns up we came down here to open the Cracker line so that our troops at Chattanooga could have something to eat but it has been so that we have had to live on half rations but we are going to have full rations tomorrow morning. the next morning after the fight we was reinforced by some of the troops from Chattanooga and General Grant made A speech to them. he told them that the Eastern boys had come down here to open The Cracker Line for them and to show them how to fight and he said that he thought that they had done it to. then they gave three cheers for General Grant and the Eastern boys and three cheers for the Cracker Line. our Division won A goof name there that night but it cost the life of many brave men. you will see A letter in the Standard in A few days that will give nearly all of the partienlars of the fight writen by Captain Shipman I think that there will be A letter in the Republican writen by someone else it is reported in camp tonight that Bragg has ordered all the sick from Chattanooga for he is A going to shell the town but I dont know whither it is so or not   if it is so there will probably be A little shelling done on both sides   Father wrote in the last letter that Mr. Scott was A going to keep the school this winter so I want you should tell him that I want that he should write to me when he gets to keeping school but I want to have him write when he has not got A bad cold. tell Mother that such Apples as they have. I pay one shilling A bushel for   up north sell for 3 for 10 cents here   that is when they can get them and Tobacco is worth about two dollars per pound and scarce at that so you see that I have to make A chew of tobacco go as far as possable and sometimes A good deal farther. when you write again send me about six stamps so that I can have some on hand. I have got 3 or 4 yet but I dont want to get out.   write often

       This from your Brother Ira

Camp of the 137th Regt. NYSV
Nov 16th 1863

Dear Parents

I have just come off from picket today and when I got to camp there was A letter for me dated the 3rd and this afternoon I receved another dated the 8th so I thought that I would try and answer them this eveing so that I could work on my tent tomorrow. we have got A good log tent almost done and have commenced to build A fire place the boys are all well what few are left with us and we had A letter today from one of the boys was getting along as well as could be expected but he did not write enny thing in partieular about them he said that Edger Elwell is expected to get A furlough soon to go home and if he does you may have A chance to see him. I dont know how bad John Thompson was wounded but I heard that it was only slightly I suppose that you had heard that Johney was Corporal he was promoted when we was at Kempers Ford Va. I have writen before what I know about the boys that was wounded so there is no use of writing about them this time   tell Father that he may send the paper again and if he can get A daily paper throw off from the cars every day I think he had better do so. I would not send for the paper enny longer but some of the boys want I should and they will send for the Standard. the captain writes for the Standard more than enny other paper now and our Ordily writes for the Republican so they want I should take that then we will get all of the letters that is writen for the papers from our Company   I shall try and write Aunt Emiline before long but I do not get much time to write and I must write home first and to others after wards. Catherine said that if I did not write to her soon she would give me A lecture but

tell her that I wrote to her about three days ago and I am A
going to write her another letter just as soon as I can get time
to write nonsence. the Rebels are on the mountain yet what
have not Deserted. there was two of our scouts came in this
morning said that the Rebs has receved reenforcements last
night so that they number about six thousand men now on
the mountain but I dont think that they will try to do enny
thing but hold the mountain. I will not write enny more to
night but I will try and write again soon.

From your son
Ira

Camp of the 137th Regt. NYSV
Nov 22th 1863

Dear Parents

It has been some time since I have receved A letter but I look for one in the next mail and as I have got time so that I can I thought I would not wate for A letter. we have got our tents about all loger up so that we are quite comfortable today is Sunday and the sun shines as bright and warm as summer I think it is likely that it is some warmer here than it is up north. the boys are all well in our company and there has been two come back that was taken prisoners at Gettysburg to our Company. the men that was taken at Gettysburg are nearly all on there way to the regiment besides A good many that have been in the Hospitals. John Thompson was wounded in the shoulder slightly he came back to the regiment the same night that I wrote my last letter to you I have not heard much from the boys that was wounded that are in the hospitals. I heard that the wounded was nearly all getting furloughs to go home tell Father that I want him to send me A pound of tobacco by the next mail for I cant get it here at enny price. some of the boys have been lucky enough to buy some once or twice but it cost them as much or more than it would to have it sent from home by mail it cost us when we can get it now about 2 dollars per pound and it is poor stuff at that so I think that I had better try and have it sent from home for I think that you can buy A better quality for 60 cents than I can for 2 dollars and it will not probably cost more than 40 cents A pound to send it by mail. I suppose that it will be so before long that we can get all we want at the old prices the Captain is with us yet but he will get away as soon as he can he is not quite as tough as

he was A year ago. it is A rough life for A man like him   if
we had never had enny more to do than the 109th regiment
has had he would have stood it first rate. but climbing over
those mountains dont agree with him   I never saw such A
country before   A man can work both sides of his farm here
but it is A rich country after all for the mountains are full
of coal mines and saltpeter works   there is some very large
caves here where they get Saltpeter. we are going to have A
meeting now so I shall have to stop writing.

This from your son
Ira S. Jeffers

Camp Near Lookout Mountain, Tenn.
December 2nd 1863

Dear Parents

We have got back to our camp again where we was when I wrote to you before. it has been some time since I have had A chance to write to you and I dont feel much like writing this morning for I am so sleepy that I can not hardly think of enny thing. I know that you anxious to hear from me. the 24th we was ordered to start from camp with one days rations and one blanket so we did not think that we could be going far for we left our tents and knapsacks and the Head Quarter Guard and pickets and one regiment from each Brigade was left. so we thought that we was only going to be gone only one day and night. but we started early on the morning of the 24th and crossed the creek and commenced to climb Lookout Mountain. we got possession of the greater part of the mountain that day and the next morning we had full possession of the mountain. the 25th we buried the dead and took care of the wounded in the afternoon. while we was A doing that there was another force engaged with the enemy on Missionary Ridge and in the afternoon our Division came around in their rear driving them and taking A good many prisoners. our Brigade was supporting there artillery so that we was not engaged. the next day we started on again after the Rebs passed over the Battle Field of Chickamauga and the 27th we was in the fight at Ringgold Ga. where we drove them again. then we had to get our wounded back to Chattanooga. we stayed there till yesterday morning then we set fire to the town and bridges and started back for this place about two o'clock in the morning. got there about dark last night. I have not wrote in my Diary about the fighting for you will see it in the papers probably before you get this. I have not heard what the loss in our regiment is yet   we did not have enny killed in our company and but three wounded   we did not have but about 15 men in the fight in our company   the rest was on picket.   the captain was not with us   he was not very well so he was left to take charge of the things that was left in camp.   we was gone about 8 days and did not have enny tents and but few had blankets   I did not have my blanket but I had my overcoat.   the nights was very cold and very heavy frosts so that we suffered considerable with cold.   so we did not get much sleep while we was gone so you can imagine about how I feel this morning   so I make some blunders in writing you need not think it strange.   Corporal Winner is well and so is Corporal Knox and I am well.   I recived A letter from you the day before we started dated the 15th and one

Battle of Lookout Mountain

at Ringgold dated the 18th and one this morning since I have been writing dated the 22th. I would have written A few lines to you while we was gone if I could have send them but A letter would not get here enny sooner that we did so I thought that I had better wait till we got back to camp then I would have A chance to write more of interest to you. you wanted to know in your letter of the 13th how I was of for clothing. I have a plenty of good cloths it has not been long since we drew clothing and I drew new shoes and stockings and as to the weather it is about as cold here at night as it is up north. we have not had menny very cold days here yet. and we dont get enny fruit we dont get enny vegetables here. but as long as they give me what hard tack and pork and coffee sugar and some times beef that I want I can get along. we have enough the most of the time and now that Chattanooga is open we will probable have enough all of the time but to tell the truth we have seen some prety short times but it was because the supplies could not get to us. we have just drawn rations two days for the last 4 days it looks rather tough but I dont know as it can be helped. I wrote for father to send me some tobacco when I wrote before and I dont want him to forget it. I bought A piece the other day of plug tobacco and gave 50 cents for it and it would take about 8 such pieces to weigh one pound and it was very poor quality at that you may think that I had better stop chewing but I had about as much chance to stop eating as to do that. it will cost more to send it by male if it is sealed up than it will if it is only tired up but I can get it cheaper eather way than I can to buy it here at this preasant time. but now that the road is opened to Chattanooga so that the sutlers can get through without much danger I think it is likely that it will be cheaper after the sutlers once get here. there has not been enny regular sutler here that I have seen yet   our sutlers that came from the Potomac with us are all back at Bridge Port, Stevenson and Nashville. there will some of them be likely to come up as soon as they can. I dont know as I can write much more this time that will be of interest to you so I will stop writing for this time.

This From Your Son
Ira

December 2 1863

Dear Parents

As I cannot send my letter till morning I thought I would write some more this afternoon. you wanted to know if I got my stamps all right. every time I think I do for I find one in every letter that you write and A sheet of paper and an envelope and I get my paper all right   the last one I got was dated the 18th   it takes them some time to get here but they are sent regular. Bob Smith has come back to the company   he went to the Hospital when we was on the march to Gettysburg and brat harriss has come back   he went to the Hospital at Nashville and there has some others came back that you are not acquained with. captain Eldrage is in command of the regiment   he had the command all through the fight. Leutenant Sage is Promoted to captain and is in command of another company. Leutenant Owen of company A had command of the two companys A and F but was killed in the commencement of the fight on Lookout Mountain so that we did not have enny company commander through the rest of the fighting. I dont know as this last sheet is very interesting so I will not write enny more at this time.

Ira

Camp of the 157 regt NyS V
December 5th 1863

Dear Sister

I recived your
letter yesterday dated Nov 23
and also the tobaco that
you sent in it whitch will
make me 5 or 6 good chews. I
have writen for father to send
me some tobaco by male
whitch I shall begin to look
for before long. you said in
your letter that if I wante
enny thing that you would
send it to me. I want som
tobaco sent by male for we
cannot get express boxes here
and I have got all the clothin
that I want now it has not
been long since we drew ou
clothing so it is nearly all ne

December 6th
Sunday morning.

I had to go
off on fatigue yesterday so
that I did not have time
to finish my letter, we
have had inspection this
morning so that we will
not have enny thing more
to do till we go to meeting
at two oclock. we have preaching nearly every Sunday
when we are in camp by
Chaplin Roberts he has
been with us ever since
the Regiment came out,
he came out with the reg-
-iment as captain and was
afterwards assined the position
of Chaplain and does the
dity of a postmaster for
the regiment too,

171

Dear Sister

I recived your letter yesterday dated Nov 23rd and also the tobacco that you sent in it whitch will make me 5 or 6 good chews. I have writen for father to send me some tobacco by male whitch I shall begin to look for before long. you said in your letter that if I wanted enny thing that you would sent it to me. I want some tobacco sent by male for we can not get express boxes here and I have got all the clothing that I want now. it has not been long since we drew our clothing so it is nearly all new. the women down here nearly all chew and smoke both and the little children use it. girls and boys both. there is A family lives near our camp here that there is A little girl between six and 7 years old that chews tobacco and snuff too. they chew the snuff here and they laugh at some of us when we told them that the women snuffed it up north. they said that that was the last way they would think of using it. you may think that I am writing what is not so but if I ever wrote the truth I am doing it now. I would not have belived it if I had been told what use they made of snuff and tobacco before I came South. when we was at Ringgold I was of the Provost Guards and it was our business to search the houses for concealed weapons and for the Rebel Soldiers that might concealed about the buildings so that I saw several pretty smart looking young ladies but all of them that I saw used tobacco eather smoked or chewed and A good manny of them done both. Just imagine how it would look for the girls up north for to chew tobacco when they was around the stove cooking and sitting in the parlors with their Beauxs on a Sunday with A great wad of tobacco in their mouth squirting tobacco juice with the energy of A steam engine. those are the southern Bells.

December 6th
Sunday morning
  I had to go off on fatigue yesterday so that I did not have time to finish my letter. we have had inspection this morning so that we will not have enny thing more to do till we go to meeting at 2 o'clock. we have preaching nearly every Sunday when we are in camp by Chaplin Roberts he has been with us ever since the Regiment came out. he came out with the regiment as captain and was afterwards assined the position of Chaplin and does the duty of A postmaster for the regiment too.
December 6th
  I thought that I would write A few more lines to you and praise your writing as well as in your studies. but I have not much of A chance to improve in writing here for I have to write on A bord on my knees and as to arithmetic I think that I can tell how much twice two is and that is about all or about how manny hard tack added together will make A meal and there I guess I am ahead of you for I dont think you can tell that. Corporal Winner and Corporal Knox are all well and I am well. I dont think of enny others in the company that you know. Johney Thompson is well I see him nearly every day his tent is opposite mine on the other side of the street so that we are only about 30 feet apart. I dont think of enny thing more in particulars to write about at preasent so I may as well bring my letter to A close for this time. but I will try and write as often as twice A week and oftener if I can. if I get A chance to write twice A week I shall think that I am doing well.

this from your Brother
Ira

Camp of the 137th Regt. NYSV
December 9th 1863

Dear Parents

I thought that I would commence to write A letter to you this morning for I am on duty so much in the day time that I dont have time to write. I wrote A letter to Catherine the 2nd and I have not receved enny letters since I got that one of Catherines but there has no mail come in today so of course I could not get enny today. there is quite A lively time here just now with the regiments that there time is nearly out enlisting again   there is several regiments in our Division that have nearly every man of them enlisted again for three years more   there is several in our regiment that will enlist for three years more now if they can get the chance. they get A 30 day furlough and 400 dollars bounty for reenlisting   I think that if they would do as well up north in Volentiering as they are doing here that we would soon get men enough in the field so that we could march right through the southern states and drive the Rebs clear into the Gulf of Mexico with out stopping. some think that the war will be done with before next spring and some think that it is just as likely to last A year or two more as enny other way but we cant tell much about it. I must put up my letter now for the Drums are beating for roll call and as soon as after that we will have to go to bed.

December 10th 1863

I am on detail here in camp today and as we have not got enny thing to do just now I thought that I would try and write A little   the mail came in this morning but I did not get A letter. there was only 3 letters for the regiment and some papers   my two last papers have not come yet but if I can get time to write I will not wate long for A letter   for I expect that there is one on the way for me and I know that you want to hear from me as often as you can. if I dont write but A few lines at A time   there is not enny news to write in particular this time   there is A good many camp rumers but they dont amount to enny thing much   some think that we will be sent back to the army of the Potomac and some says that Geary has telegraphed to Washington for permission to let his division all go home for 60 days. but it is nothing but camp rumor so we dont put much confidence in it. although we was the First Division on Lookout Mountain.   Milt and Bob are both well and I am well   I will write again as soon as I get A letter if it is tomorrow.

This from your son

Ira

Camp of the 137th reg NYSV
December 12th 1863

Dear Parents

    I received A letter from you today dated the 2nd and last night I got my paper dated the 2nd and also A note from the Postmaster at Nashville saying that there was A letter detained in that office bearing my address and that I could have it by returning the note and enclosing one stamp for non payment of postage. so I sent back the note today. I cannot see to write very well this evening but I thought that I would try and answer your letter as soon as I could. I have not received Mr. Sealts letter yet   the mail dont come very regular   I wrote for Father to send me some tobacco by mail before the fight on Lookout Mountain but you did not mention it in your last letter so I think that it must be that you have not got that letter yet. I dont think that you get all of my letters so I will number them for A spell and see how you get them then you can tell whether there is enny that you dont get or not. the 29th Pa Volunteers went home to day   they have enlisted again for three years more and are to have A furlough for 30 days but they will probably be there longer than that to get recruits to fill up there regiment to A full number.

December 13th

    it is sunday today and it is wet rainy day. it is as warm as A spring morning   we do not have much cold weather here. I wrote A letter to you the 10th for I did not know how long it might be before I would get A letter from you and I like to write often when I can get time. I have not much news to write   we are lying in the same place that we have been since we first came here. we are about 6 miles from Chattanooga. there is A detail from our regiment every day to work on the road on Lookout Mountain that goes to Chattanooga. we dont get much of the war news here the most of the papers that we get is our Binghamton paper Tell Catherine that the tobacco that she sent me was the best that I have tasted in A long time and if Father dont send me some that she may send some in her letters. Milt Knox and Bob Winner are both well and I am well but tell Catherine that I dont know how much I weigh now I will try and find out when I write to her again. I cant think of much more to write and what I have wrote dont amount to much so I might as well stop writing for this time.

This From Your Son
Ira S. Jeffers

Dear Parents

I receved A letter from you this afternoon dated the 6th so I thought that I would try and answer it this evening for I expect to be on detail tomorrow again so that I would not have A chance to write then. seargant Frank Newman of company "B" died yesterday morning at the Regimental hospital and was burried today his folks live where Solaman used to live near the schoolhouse. I was acquainted with him before he enlised and have been to the same school with him A good many days he was expecting A furlough to go home in A day or two. it is the first death that has been in the regiment in A long time by disease but there has been A good many killed in battle since we have been here in the Western Army. Milt Knox and Bob Winner are both well we are lying near Chattanooga where we was before the fight and have got good tents built of logs and covered with our shelter tents and have got A good fire place in it so that we are quite comfortable. there is no use of your trying to send me enny thing only what you send by mail. we cannot get things here as we could in the Army of the Potomac we could get express boxes there but we cannot get them here for it is all they can do to get our rations to us. we have not drawn full rations in A good while but we have not suffered very bad yet for provisions there was A time before the fight that we had to live mostly on pop corn for two or three days but that was better than to be A prisoner on Belle Island. we was thankful for what we did receve and tobacco is very scarce here and even if there was tobacco enough here it would be hard for A good many to buy it for they are mostly all out of money. we expected to have got our pay some time ago but we will have to wate now till we are mustered again   I will not write enny more tonight but if I can get A chance to write some more tomorrow before the mail goes out I will do so.

December 16th 1863
I am not on detail as yet this morning   so as soon as I get done writeing I shall try and mend my clothes some. I have got my old diary yet but it is hardly worth sending home but I think that I will send it and if you are A mind to you may send me another. I shall nor send this one yet   in two or three weeks   I have receved (not) Mr. Scotts letter yet nor the one detained in the office at Nashville   we have had men enough come back from the hospital so that we have got A prety good company. now we have got 28 men and there is about two hundred fifty men in the regiment now. I have about filled up my sheet so I will not write enny more this time.

Ira S. Jeffers

Camp of the 137th Regt. N.Y.S.V.
December 20th 1863

Dear Parents

I think it is about time for me to write again   I have not receved A letter from you since the 15th and I answered it the 16th   I look for A letter every time the mail comes in but I know well enough that I wont get one every day. we dont get much war news here but it is the general opinion among the men that the war is about over for this time but I have got A kind of an idea that the men that are enlisting over again for three years more will be likely to see Mexico before there next three years are over but if peace is restored between the North and the South this winter I dont think but what Uncle Sam can raise another Vollentier Army next fall if he should need them to help Mexico. there was another regiment from our Division that has enlisted for three years more and they went home yesterday   it was the 66th Ohio regiment. our regiment will not be very likely to enlist over for we have not been two years in the field yet so we will not be allowed to. it would be paying us rather to much bounty they keep us prety busy building cordaroy roads just now. but we will soon have the road done that we are at work at now. then I suppose we will have to go to work on the rail road.

December 24th 1863

I did not have A chance to finish my letter till today and I may be called on some detail before I get it finished this time. the 60th regt. NYSV are going home and they have called for pickets from our regiment to relive there men that are on picket. they have enlisted for three years more so when they leave we will not have but 4 regiments left in our Brigade. we have got the cordaroy road done that we was to work on.

it was only three miles from Division Head Quarters to the Landing and it took the teams 2 days to go there and back before we fixed the road and they said that as soon as we got the road done that we would draw full rations but we dont seem to get them yet. we draw full rations of Pork three quarters rations of hard bread but it is not more than half rations. I have bought A good many Hard Tack if I had not bought enny I should have went hungry A good share of the time. I could buy them for 5 cents per pound and as long as I could do that I was not A going hungry and when you write again I would like to have you send me one dollar and no more. my health is good I have not felt better since I have been in the service.

This from your son
Ira

Camp near Chattanooga Tenn.
December 28th 1863

Dear Parents

I receved the tobacco that you sent me last Saturday all right and also the letter that Catherine wrote to me the 16th but I have not got the letter that Mr. Scott wrote nor the one that was detained in the Post Office in Nashville so I have about made up my mind that that is the one that Mr. Scott wrote. I should have wrote to you the next day after I got your letter but I had to go to Head Quarters Guard so I had to wate till today to write. I feel prety good over my tobacco you sent me just the kind I wanted we are expecting to march in A day or two we are going back on the rail road some where near Stevenson to guard the rail road I suppose. our Division has nearly all relisted and are going home nearly every day there is but 4 regiments in our Brigade now and two of them have inlisted again and are expecting to start for home in A day or two and those in the regiment that are reenlisting that dont enlist are put in the regiments that are left to serve out the rest of their time. I cannot write much this time for it is nearly night and we are drawing rations so that I have to write between calls. I dont know when we will leave here it may be tomorrow and it may not be in A week but I think it will be as soon as the weather gets to be A little better. we dont get much war news so I cannot write enny. Milt Knox and Bob Winner are both well and I am well. I will not write enny more for now but I will try and write some more before the mail goes out tomorrow.

December 29th 1863

I will try and finish my letter this morning. I have not got much news to write   there was one man yesterday that had his head shaved and was drumed out of camp for Cowardice at the battle of Lookout Mountain. but I do not want that kind of A Discharge and I dont think that there is many that does. I suppose that Captain Shipman will leave us soon or in A short time. he has got A position of some kind in Washington so that he will get out of the fighting department. but I think that the fighting must be about played out now.

Ira S. Jeffers

Camp Near Chattanooga
December 31st 1863

Dear Parents

I recived A letter from you today dated the 13th and I got one from Catherine dated the 16th last Saturday and the Tobacco that father sent to me. So this letter has been some time comming but it is new for all that. it is wet rainy weather here now but we have got good comfortable quarters but we expect to have to leave them soon. I suppose that we will go back on the Railroad to join the rest of the Corp. but there is not more that one small Division left of the Corps for nearly all of the old regiments have enlisted over for three years and gone home. so I do not know what will be done with the Remander of the corp. I think it will be ether filled up or else we will be consoladated with some other corps. there is some talk of giving our Regiment A chance to reenlist and if they do we will have to serve three years and A half making 5 years in all the same as other Regiments but I dont much think it will be done. we have had about 30 recruits come into our regiment. then that was left that did not reenlist of the old regiment.

Tell father that I would like to have him send me A Diary. Milt had one sent to him and the postage on it was only 4 cents and it was A large one too. I want one that has about two days on one page. I wrote for you to send me one dollar but if you have not sent it before you get this letter you need not sent it for we expect to be paid now in A few days and if we are I shall not need it. the Captain says that we will be paid tomorrow but we may not be paid till after we move. the mail will not go out till tomorrow so I will wate till then to finish my letter.

Your Son
Ira S. Jeffers

1864

Duty at Bridgeport until May

Atlanta Georgia Campaign May 1 – September 8
Demonstration on Rocky Faced Ridge, May 8 – 11
Battle of Resaca, May 14 – 15
Near Cassville, May 19
Advance on Dallas, May 22 – 25
New Hope Church, May 25
Battles about Dallas, New Hope Church and Allatoona Hills, May 26 – June 5
Operations about Marietta and against Kenesaw Mountain, June 10 – July 2
Pine Hill, June 11 – 14
Lost Mountain, June 15 – 17
Gilgal or Golgotha Church, June 15
Muddy Creek, June 17
Noye's Creek, June 19
Kolb's Farm, June 22
Assault on Kenesaw, June 27
Ruff's Station, Smyrna Camp Ground, July 4
Chattahoochee River, July 5 – 17
Peach Tree Creek, July 19 - 20
Siege of Atlanta, July 22 – August 25
Operations at Chattahoochee River Bridge, August 26 – September 2
Occupation of Atlanta, September 2 – November 15
Expedition to Tuckum's Cross Roads, October 26 – 29
Near Atlanta, November 9

March to the sea November 15 – December 10
Near Davisboro, November 28
Siege of Savannah, December 10 - 21

Camp near Chattanooga
January 3rd 1864

We did not get our pay as I expected and the next day I had to go on guard so that I did not have A chance to write enny more till today. we have just signed the payrolls   later we have drew our pay for two months. I got A check for 10 dollars and one dollar and 99 cents. the rest was taken out to pay for the clothing that I drew more that was allowed by the government. inclosed you will find the check of 10 dollars   I receved A letter from you yesterday dated the 21st and I got Mr. Sealts letters yesterday. it was detained in Nashville   I will answer it as soon as I can.

Ira

January 3rd

We are expecting to start for Bridge Port in the morning so it may be some time before I can get A chance to answer Mr. Seals letter but I will answer it as soon as I can and I will answer yours as soon as Possibable.

1) Stevenson Alabama
January 8th 1864

Dear Parents

We have moved from where we was when I wrote to you before. we are now at Stevenson doing guard duty   our Corps is station all along the rail road from Bridgeport to Nashville and our Brigade is at this place what is left of it there is but two regiments of it left the rest have reenlisted and gone home   I wrote A letter to you the day before we left Chattanooga and put A check of ten dollars in it but you may not get it in some time for I gave it to the Chaplin and he is

A going home and will put it in A mail office there. we drew two months pay but it took 14 dollars and 5 cents to pay for my clothing that I had drawn more than the government allows. Captain Shipman has resinged and will probably be at home before you get this   he left us the night before we started from our old camp   I receved A letter from you dated the 27th of December and also the diary that Father sent   I wrote for him to send A larger one then the last time I wrote to you but this is larger enough to carry in my pocket.   I think that I like it better than I would A larger one   I got the Scotts letter just before we left our old camp but I have not had A chance to answer it yet but I will do so as soon as I can. one was detained in the post office at Nashville for some time   it had one two cent stamp on it and I should think by the look of it that there had been another one on it and it had come off. so it cost me two stamps besides one envelope but I was glad to get it at that   when you write again send me two two cent stamps so that I can send the old diary   I am afraid that it will not go through without enny stamps on it. Ed Elwell has not got here yet nor I have not heard from him he has probable stopped at the hospital. Milt Knox   Bob Winner and Johney Thompson are well and I am well   we was all prety stiff and sore when we got here but are getting about over it now.   you need not send the stamps that I spoke about for I have traded A three cent stamp for some one cent stamps and I will send the diary in the same mail with this letter. it does not look every well but it did till the Gettysburg march than I sweat so that it was nearly spolit. I can not see to write very well this evening so I will not try to write enny longer.

This from your son
Ira

Stevenson Ala.
January 10th 1864

Dear Sister

I recived your letter last night dated Jan. 3rd. I wrote A letter to mother the 8th so I have not got much news to write this time. we are doing Guard duty here at this place now and I expect that we shall stay here some time. it is prety cold weather here now but I dont think it will last as long as it does up North. I got my Diary all right and it suits me first rate and I have sent home my old one. I did not keep it very good but I will try and do better with this one. I have not seen enny of the Boys that have started to come down here to work. only John Whitney Pat Whitneys Brother. I saw him at shell Mound. the Boys that come to work on the railroad will probably go on down nearly to Chattanooga so that I will not be likely to see them unless it is when they pass through here we are on the same road that they will be at work on so I will be likely to see some of them after A while. Bill Smith had A letter from Charley Stringham yesterday he wrote that he was well. I shall try and write A letter to him soon if I get time after I have answered Mr. Sealts letter and I mean to try and do that to day. our Ordily Sergant Wellman went home on A furlough about the time that we left our old camp he was sick and had been for some time with Chromic Diarhea. that is A disease that is not very easily cured in the army but if they can get you home where they can get such food as they want it is not so hard to cure it. but manny times in the army the sick have to eat about the same kind of food that they did when they was well. there in not manny sick in the regiment now. Milton Knox Robert H. Winner Johney Thompson and my self are well at preasent and I think the company is all enjoying A prety good degree of health at preasent.

Jan. 12th 1864

Dear Sister

I was detailed on guard the next morning after I commenced to answer your letter so I did not have A chance to finish it till this morning. I have commenced to answer Mr. Sealts letter and shall try and finish it this morning. the Boys are all well I believe this morning. I have not seen enny of the boys yet that you said was comming down here to work on the Rail Road. our guard duty is prety strict here and our Regiment is the Provost Guard and we have got A Brass Band now. it is A Brigade Band. we have not had one before.

Ira

Send me some stamps when you write again for I have not got but one left.

1) Stevenson Ala.
January 13th 1864

Dear Parents

I receved your letter this evening dated the 6th of January with the money in it   we have been paid off   we got two months pay. I got A check of 10 dollars and one dollar and 35 cents in money   the rest of the two months pay had to go to pay for clothing that I had drew more than was allowed by the government and some of the boys had to pay for clothing that we are prety sure that they never drew but I cant say as I did and this year I shall keep my clothing account my self then I shall be perfectly satisfide for they cant compel me to sign the clothing roll. they can prove that I have had the clothing but I think I have had all the clothing that was charged to me. I got my tobacco before we left our camp near Chattanooga and my diary I got after we got here but I had kept the days all noted down on paper so it is just as well as though I had got it New Years day and my old diary I sent home and I have sent the check. the weather has been prety cold here for A spell but today it is all most as warm as spring. we had some snow on New Years for the first time so the ground was just about as white as A good frost would make it. it has snowed A little once since but it did not last long I have not seen enny of the boys that have come down to work yet. it may be that they passed through here in the night for they will probably go down nearly to Chattanooga for there is not much to be done to the railroad till they get the other side of Bridgeport and it may be that they have not passed through here yet and I dont think that they have. Milton Knox Robert H. Winner are all well. I have not seen Johney Thompson today but I did yesterday he was well then and I am well I finished A letter yesterday that I was writing to Catherine and put it in the office and answered Mr. Scotts letter. I answered his just as soon as I could after answering yours I though that you had the first claim I wrote A good long one but I dont know as there was much in it that would be interesting to him. I have no more room on this sheet so I will close.

This from your son

Ira

Stevenson Ala.
January 19th 1864

Dear Parents

The Chaplain was going home today and said if we had enny thing that we wanted to send home he would take it for us. so I have sent my Watch by him. it is all right but the katch that holds it when you wind it that is wore so that it dont hold and the crystal is broken out   I have never had one in it since I got it   I cant write much for I have not got time.

Ira.

Stevenson Ala.
January 20th 1864

Dear Parents

I have not receved A letter from you since the 13th and I did not want to send A letter without A stamp on it so I thought that I would wate A spell for A letter. I look for one in the morning. I shall go on guard in the morning so that I will not have much time to write tomorrow and I thought that I might as well commence my letter this afternoon then I could finish it in the morning. I come on guard nearly every other day so it keeps me prety buisy. I came off from guard this morning and since that we have washed our clothes I carried water and the other two boys done the washing. the Chaplin went home yesterday and I sent my watch by him he will leave it in the Post Office at Binghamton. tell Father that if it dont cost to much to get it fixed. or if he can sell it for 10 dollars to let it go. that is before he gets it fixed. it was A good watch for time after I had it cleaned at Kempers Ford till after the fight on Lookout Mountain then the Katch got so that it would not hold when I went to wind it. and I got A watch tinker that was in the Regiment to fix it but it did not stay fixed two days. tell Father to do what he is A mind to with it. if he get it fixed and dont sell it I may send for it again. there has some of the boys passed through here from Binghamton but I did not see enny that I knew Gil Hausbrook was among them but I did not see him Bob seen him and said that he inguired for me. Milt Knox Bob Winner Johney Thompson and myself are all well at present. and I dont hear of menny sick in the Regiment and belive that there is not enny sick in our company now. you have probably seen Captain Shipman before this time. but Cap Shipman no more. he left us without enny company Commander I was not sorry when he left only I would liked to have had him stayed till Sage got back to take command of us so that they could not have put an officer over us out of some other company.

Ira

Jan. 21th /64

There was no letters come this morning so of course I did not get enny. but I will finish my letter and send it. then I will write again as soon as I do get one. I am on guard again today as usual but it is easy work and I like it. it is very pleasant weather here now. it is as warm today as summer up North. some nights it is quite cold so that the ground will be frozen quite hard in the morning. but I suppose that there is good sleighing up North now. Ed Elwell has not got here yet nor I have not heard where he is. he has stopped at some hospital I think or he would have been here. I want that you should write as soon as you get the watch and what Father thinks of it. and write if you got the Diary. I like my little Diary first rate. it is just large enough and so far I have kept every day wrote full. I would like to have you send me some stamps for if we stay here long I shall have time to write considerable besides what I write home. I will not write enny more now for it is time to eat my Dinner and we have A good Bean Soup for dinner.

This from your son
Ira S. Jeffers

1) Stevenson Ala.
January 22th 1864

Dear Parents

I receved your letter this morning dated the 10th and I wrote A letter to you yesterday   so that I have not got much news to write today. I could have sold A part of my tobacco when we was at Chattanooga but we have got where we can get tobacco cheaper than we could there and besides that we can send to Nashville by some of the Engineers or other boys that are on the cars and get it as cheap as you can send it from home. the money that you sent in the other letter comes pretty good for I did not get but one dollar and 35 cents besides the check when we drew our pay. I have got 9 plugs of my tobacco left yet   tell Grandmother that we get enough to eat here now. we have warm bread every morning from the bakery and good Pork coffee sugar and sometimes Beans   sometimes we buy flour and we make flour gravy whitch makes pretty good liveing   in my letter yesterday I wrote to you about my watch so there is no use of my writeing about it today. the Chaplin will leave it in the

Post Office at Binghamton so you can get it about as soon as you get this letter.

January 23th

I am not on guard today so I have been to work cleaning my gun and now I will try and finish my letter. I wrote for you to send me some stamps in my other letter and I wished you would   then I can write A good many letters for I have got paper and envelopes enough to last sometime with what you send me   there is A good many that I would like to write to now that we are in camp so that I can. the boys are all well today   Johney said that he has not had A letter from home lately but I guess he dont get as many as I do. our Seargant says that I get A letter in almost every mail with the same hand writeing on the same kind of an envelope. I cannot think of enny thing more to write at present. so I will close and go and get some wood for night.

This from your son
Ira.

P.S. I have sent you A letter from Captain Shipman and one from another Captain in this letter.

Jan. 29th 1864

Dear Sister

I receved your letter today of the 17th and lose no time in answering it. yesterday I receved A letter from Wallace and day before yesterday I receved one from Uncle George and answered it today   we are having very pleasant weather here it is as warm as the days in spring at home   I am on guard nearly every other day and is light so it is not very hard work. I was weighted the other day and I weighted 143 lbs. and I dont think that you weight much more than that. you wrote about your spelling School so I will write about the schools we have   we have got A old spelling book and every night there will be 4 or 5 of us in our tent and spell for A hour or two. we have sent for A speller and definer whitch we expect will be here soon and I think that we have improved conciderable since we began. I think it is about as good A way as we can find to spend our evenings. I have not got much news to write for I dont hear much war news   you have A better chance to hear that than I do unless it is something that happens near where I am. the Regiment is in execllent health   the Doctor said he never saw it better. Bob Winner and Milt Knox and Johney Thompson are all well. the Sanitary Commisson are building over the Alabamma House and fitting it up for A soldiers home so that the soldiers will not have to lay out in the cold when they are detained here over night. we have got good comfortable quarters here and I should not be supprized if we stayed here quite A spell but we cant tell what we may do. we have got an old church for A prison house and have on an average about 50 men in it and sometimes A hundred. we have Rebs and Union prisoners Deserters and all such men. some of them we have got A chain and iron ball fasten on there legs   the balls weight between 30 and 40 pounds we keep our guns loaded when on guard and have orders to shoot enny one that we see trying to escape if we cannot stop them without   I have not seen enny of the boys that I know that have passed through here yet but there is another train comming through here today and I may know some of them. I will not write enny more this time.

From your Brother
Ira.

Stevenson Ala
January 31th 1864

Dear Parents

I recived your letter this morning dated the 24th and was glad to hear that you was all well and that you had recived the Diary. the boys are all well except Captain Sage   he is verry sick now with A fever so that he is out of his head. there has not enny of our regiment reenlisted. the Ordily seargent was sick and went home on A furlough. we get A plenty to eat here it is coffee sugar pork beans and soft bread. we draw our bread every morning at the Bakery. then we buy flour and make flour gravy. I think the Chaplin kept the check till he went home is the reason why you have not got it yet and I have sent my watch home by him   he will leave it at the post office in Binghamton so that you can get it. we are guarding Government stores and Prisoners   we have got an old church for A prison house and we have from 50 to 100 in it at A time   Rebel prisoners and deserters from our army   men in there for almost all kinds of offences and some of them have got an iron ball and chain fastened to their legs. besides some rebel officers that we have got in another building separate from the rest.

I am on guard nearly every other day so that I have one night to sleep and the next night I can only sleep A part of the time. but that is all we have to do is guard duty. the report in camp to day is that they have been fighting at Know Ville for A day or two but I have not seen it in the papers yet. the rebels keep comeing into our lines and A good menny of them are inlisting in our cavalry. some of the prisoners think Nepolian will recognise the Southern Confederacy so that they will gain their independence yet. they think that we cant fight them both and others think that they are about played out. It is reported now that there has been another division added to our corps whitch begins to make the boys think that we are to take to the field of operations again as soon as spring and that they will put some of the new troops on the railroad. but time will show. they was down on us when we first came here those western troops. but they seem to like the looks of the stars now at least there is A good manny of them that wear them.

Feb 1th

there was A train came in yesterday with some of the workmen on that I knew. I saw frank tyler and tom swan.

Ira

Feb 1st 1864

Dear Father

I saw Ira Hawly this morning he has come down here to work on the railroad. he sends his best respects to you and wanted that I should write and ask you if you remember the

Gray horse that he traded you. he says he did skim you on the trade. I dont know why it is but I have not seen enny one of them yet that knew me till I told them who I was. Tom Swan did not know me till after I told him who I was. Tom Eggleston was sick and John Eggleston stoped to take care of him so I have not seen him yet. I have not got much news to write I am on guard again to day. Corporal Winner and Corporal Knox is well and so am I. the weather is warm and pleasant although it rained quite hard last night it has about dried off the boys think that the weather is some different from what it is up north. I will have to stop writing now so as to get my dinner before I go on guard again.

This from your Son
Ira

Stevenson Ala.
Feb 7th 1864

Dear Parents

It has been one week ago today since I have receved A letter from you and I thought that I would be shure to get one yesterday or to day if you wrote A Sunday as you generalry do. I should have written before this time if I had had enny stamps but I will send it without A stamp this time rather than wait enny longer. Milt Knox Bob Winner Johney Thompson and my self are all well. Captain Sage is getting better. we had A letter yesterday from one of the boys that is in the hospital and he says that Ed Elwell is there sick with the small Pox. we like our Guard duty here first rate we are on guard prety often but we get A plenty to eat we bought some potatoes the other day enough for three or four good meals and we traded some coffee with some of the citizens for some Indian meal and last night we traded some more coffee for some milk so we had A good suppire of pudding and milk. it is not often that enny of the inhabitants have enny thing of that kind to sell for the government has to support the most of them. they come from ten to 15 miles here after rations and clothing. there is not menny men   they are mostly all women and children   their husbands are eather in the Rebel army or the union army but they are mostly in the Rebel army.

Tell Catherine that when she has enny papers or magizines with enny good stories in them to send them to me after she has read them for I want some things to read and it will not cost but two cents to send them and they would be worth ten times that to me. I had rather sit down in my tent and read than be running around in the streets. we do as A general thing have A spelling school in our tent almost every evening whitch I think has been some benifit to us. Hiram Bullock has been transferred to the invilid corps so one of the boys wrote from Nashville   it is getting dark so I will not write enny more this time. I will answer your letter as soon as I get it and it must be on the way somewhere.

This From Your Son
Ira S. Jeffers

Soldier reading newspaper

Stevenson Ala.
Feb. 9th 1864

Dear Parents

I receved your letter this morning dated the 31th of Jan. and it was not mailed till the 3rd of Feb. I did not know but what you had forgotten me for it has been almost ten days since I have receved A letter from you. I do not know where the Chaplin lives but I belive he lives in Newark where George used to live but he said that he should go to Binghamton. if Father gets the watch fixed and dont sell it right off I think that I shall send for it again. the 66th Ohio regiment that reenlisted when we was at Wauhatchie Valley has got back. Ed Elwell is at Nashville sick with the Small Pox but we have heard that he is getting better. Hiram Bullock has been transfered to the Invalid Corps. so he will not be with us in the regiment enny more but the rest of the boys that you know I think is well. Milt Knox Robert Winner Johney Thompson and my self are all well. there is Rebel Prisoners passing through nearly every day yesterday there was about 300 three hundred went through on one train they deserting all of the time just as fast as they can and not yet catched. I have just eat my dinner whitch consisted of nicely cooked beans and soft Bread and all the fault that I have to find with my dinner is that I have to eat to much for comfort. I received my paper this morning dated the 3rd of Feb. it is about all that I get to read I wrote in my last letter for Catherine to send me some things to read I would not care if the papers was 3 years old if they only had some good storys in them I have had A letter from Uncle George since we have been here and have answered it. and one from Wallace I answered his yesterday and I am going to write one to Aunt Malvina just as soon as I can convienantly. I would like to have you send me A pair of stockings half cotton and if you can send them by mail for about 4 cents if they are done up in A strong package. these Government socks wear out so soon   Milt had two pair and they wore as long as A half dozen of the government stockings.   I have not enny thing more to write this time so I will close this.

From your son
Ira.

Stevenson, Ala.
Feb 11th /64

Dear Parents

I received your letter this morning dated the 3rd of February and mailed the 4th, and received on the 9th and answered it the same day. we dont have much war news here now but they are fixing for a campaign in the spring they are sending Altillery to the front nearly all the time and they are fixing up old wagons and building new ones all of the time   I heard some of them telling that they had got to have 400 ready by the first of march. So they will probably be doing something about that time. the Veteran Soldiers are beginning to come back again. Tell Catherine that I did not try to do the example that she sent for I did not think that I could do it   if I did try so I thought that I might better be mending my clothes than be wasting my time on it. Tell Grandmother that I cannot think of enny funny stories to write to her but if I was there I could tell some stories

Wagons waiting to be repaired

that would be quite interesting whither they was verry funny or not. you must know that I have traveled some since I left home and have seen A good deal and have been in 10 different States besides the District of Colombia where the Capital of the United States is situated.

I had to stop writing and get dinner for the other boys that was on guard. we take turns at cooking there is 3 of us that tent together and there is not but two of us on guard at one time. I came off from guard this morning and they went on. I had A good dinner of fresh beef and potatoes and soft bread. we have more coffee that we want to use so we sell it to the citizens for the money then we buy potatoes from the commissaries and our coffee money almost pays for them. so we are just living off from the top self. we have drawn potatoes once since we have been here. I think the reason why you have not got the Watch and check is because the Chaplin has not been to Binghamton yet he probably went home first. I think that you will get them all right after A while and as soon as you get them write and let me know I think if it dont cost more than one dollar or ten shillings that he had better get it fixed for it has kept good time till it got out of Repair. Milt Knox and Bob Winner and myself are all well. no more this time.

This from your Son
Ira

Stevenson Ala.
Febuary 13th 1864

Dear Parents

We drew our pay yesterday of two months whitch was 26 dollars   we did not get enny checks this time but I shall send just the same amount as though we did   I will send ten dollars in this letter and next time I will send ten more. I have just been to the express office to see how much it would cost to send it by express and they was A going to charge me one dollar for sending 20 and I thought that I had rather risk it by mail than pay the price they said. the boys are all well at present   I want that you should write just as soon as you get this even if you have just writen the day before. I have not got enny news to write this time and it has not been A day or two since I have wrote. so no more this time.

This from your son
Ira S. Jeffers

Stevenson Ala.
Feb. 15th 64

Dear Parents

The Chaplin has got back. he did not go to Binghamton for when he got home his family was sick so he stayed at home and sent the Watch by express. so if you have not got it yet you had better have Father go to the express office and see if he can find it there. it is directed to you. it is an replacement watch hunter case silver and has been galvinised on the inside of the cases   the crystal has been broke out. and the ketch is so that it will not hold when you go to wind it. I wrote A letter to you day before yesterday and sent ten dollars in it and will send ten more just as soon as I get A letter from you. we did not draw enny Checks this time but I shall send the same amount that the Checks would have been. I commenced to write A letter to Aunt Malaina yesterday and shall try and finish it today. I belive I have not wrote to her since we have been in the western army. I have wrote so often this week that I shall not write much this time.

This from your son
Ira S. Jeffers

Stevenson, Ala.
Feb. 17th /64

Dear Parents

I recived your letter of the 7th. It was mailed the 9th. And I got it yesterday. I wrote A letter to you the other day to let you know where I thought the watch was. I think it is in the express office. the Chaplin did not go to Binghamton so he sent it by express. our ordily has got back he got here this morning. they are giving out more furloughs now and John Hanley is to have one. he tents with me so I shall not send the rest of the money till he goes home then I will send it by him and have him leave it in the Post Office at Binghamton. and if you want to send some things to me he will bring them but he cannot bring much for he has got to bring some things for the rest of the boys. he lives on Syracuse Earl road in A little white house on the same road that comes out by Andersons Grocery on the canal. the last that I heard from Ed Caldwell he was getting better. they are not vaccinating enny of the soldiers here and there is no cases of the small pox here. all of our company are well at present with the exception of two or three that have got hard colds whitch we must expect this time of the year. the weather has been verry cold for two or three days so that it made me think of the cold weather up North. but the citizens say it is the coldest winter that has been here in several years. if you dont get that check before you get this letter just look in my Diary and find the date and number of it and send it to me so that I can try and get another check when we are paid again. for I dont want both the watch and check to get lost. I went to the express office to see about sending my money this time and they was A going to charge me one dollar to send 20 so I thought that I would risk it to go by mail but if I lose it this time I will send it by express next time I think. But if John gets his furlough I shall send ten dollars by him so that that you will get that much all right. I will not write enny more for this time for I have just came off from guard and am some sleepy.

This from your Son
Ira S. Jeffers

Stevenson Ala.
Feb. 23th, 64

Dear Parents

I recived your letter this morning of the 15th and was glad to hear that you was all well. I am well and so are the rest of the boys from Port Crane. we remain hear yet at Stevenson doing guard duty. but the main army are on the move. the Rebel Morgin is said to be prowling around in this vicinity. and we have been under arms twice expecting an attack and it was in the night both times but so far we have not been molested. but dont know how soon we may be. John Hanleys furlough has not come yet but he is expecting it now every day and when he gets home he says that he will go to my house then you can have A good chance to hear from me. and have A chance to send some things by him. I shall send 10 dollars by him and with the ten that I have send will amount to the same that the check would. I want father to get me A new watch. Patent Lever hunter case worth between 16 or 18 dollars and sell the one that I send home and I will send him enough of my spending money with what he gets for the old one to pay for it. and John will bring it to me if he gets it. I think that the check and watch must be in the express office at Binghamton but if they are not there I will speak to the Chaplin about them and see if he cannot find out where they are. but I want father to get me A new watch whether he gets the other one or not and I will try and pay for it and send home my ten dollars A month besides. I may just as well spend my 3 dollars A month for that as enny thing else. I have not had much time to write lately or I should have writen to you before this time. but I intented to write to you to day whether I got A letter or not.

I would have my likeness taken and send by John but there is no artist here so I will have to wate till some other time. I shall have to stop writing now for the mail will go out in A short time.

This from your Son
Ira S. Jeffers

Stevenson Ala.
Feb 27th 1864

Dear Parents

I receved your letter this morning of the 19th but I have not got the stockings yet. I receved the stamps all right and also those that you sent before I wrote to you that I thought that the watch was at the express office but you did not write whether you have looked there for it or not so I think that you have not got that letter yet. the Army at the front is on the move and have been fighting some so that John Hanly will not get his furlough quite yet for we shall want all of our men here on the railroad till this movement is over. we are not troubled much about the caverly that was around here A few days ago. it is said to have been but A small force and has entirely disapaired I think that I shall not wait for John to send my money. as soon as I hear about the ten dollars that I have sent then I will send the other ten. I wrote A letter to Aunt Malvina the 14th. she will probably get it as soon as she gets home I shall have to get ready for dress parade. I will finish in the morning.

Feb 28th 1864

I receved your letter this morning dated the 20th in whitch you said that you had got the ten dollars that I sent so I will send ten more in this one for John will not get his furlough very soon and I dont want to be bothered with it enny longer. the socks have not come yet when we was at Gettysburg I lost my knapsack and all of the things that I had in it but my silk hankerchief that I had in my pocket so I have got that yet. but before I left the battlefield I picked up another knapsack that had about as much in it as mind did and A good needle book with plenty of thread in it. I have not got my paper yet but the other boys got theirs two or three days ago   it has not come very regular lately   we drew some socks the other day so you need not send enny more just now. the boys are all well and I am well   I think that we will be here all summer if the Small Pox dont break out here   one of the boys in the regiment has got the measels but he is getting better   I will put ten dollars in this letter and write as soon as you get it.

This from your son
Ira S. Jeffers

Stevenson Ala.
Feb 28th 1864

Dear Brother

I thought that as you was kind enough to write to me that I would write to you. I think that you are getting to be A prety good writer and if you keep on you will soon get so that you will beat me. you must write to me as often as you can and when you write again tell me what you have done with the old fiddle and whether you have got so that you can play enny on it or not. there is some talk of giveing our regiment A chance to reenlist next march but I dont know whether I shall reenlist or not. Tell Father that I want that he should have all of your Photographs taken and send to me he can send them in the letters one at A time. I have got Grandfathers yet and it is just as nice as it was when I first got it. I would have my likeness taken again now if there was enny place to and send it home. I cannot think of enny thing more to write this time so I will have to stop for this time.

From Ira S. Jeffers
To his Brother
"Albert"

Stevenson Ala.
March 5th /64

Dear Parents

    I recived your letter this morning of the 25th in whitch you said that you had got my watch and check all right. I had almost made up my mind that you would not get them at all. I sent 10 dollars the 29th and shall look for an answer about A week from today. that will make 20 dollars that I have sent since we have been here at Stevenson. Captain Eldrage has been promoted to Major and is coming home to get recrutes. he is going to start today so he said this morning. you may see him before he comes back if we stay where we are now he will probably stay up north some time. I cannot write very well today for we are drawing rations and I have to keep getting up to drew mine besides I am cooking beans whitch takes A good share of my attention. I got A letter from Afretia the other day and have commenced to answer it but I thought that I would answer yours first. the regiments that reenlisted and went home have all come back but one of our Brigade and they will probably be back before long. I have got A song that one of the boys in our Brigade got up about our fight in Wauhatchie Lookout Mountain and Missionary Ridge that I will send in this letter. I think that they are prety well got up. and it is about as near the truth as they could get it. I cannot write much more at this time that will be interesting so I might as well stop. Milt Knox Bob Winner Johney Thompson and my self are all well. so far since we have been here it has been prety healthy. no more at preasant.

Ira S. Jeffers

I recived my stockings all right.

Stevenson, Ala.
March 10th 1864

Dear Parents

I recived your letter this morning of the 1st and will lose no time in answering it. the Boys are all well at preasant and I am well. tell father that I dont want an open face watch for if I should break the crystal I might not be where I could get one in again in six months and with A hunter case it would not make much difference. but I dont see enny chance for getting one sent yet for the furloughs are suspended for the preasant so I dont know when John will get his Furlough. I think that you had better sell the one that I sent home. and buy a new one and keep it A spell till you see whether it will run good or not and probably be that time there will be some chance to send it. I suppose it could be sent by express. but if we should happen to move it might trouble me to get it. I have got my stockings all right. if I thought that we should get our pay again soon I would send some more money to father. I sent 10 dollars the 29th of last month. you will probably get it some time before you get this letter. when you write again write how much money you have recived from me so as to know if you have recived all that I have sent. I have sent $152. one hundred and fifty two dollars but I dont think there has been enny of it lost. Bill Smith had A letter from Ed Elwell the other day. he is in the Hosptal at Nashville yet and is getting better. I can not write enny more this time for the mail will go out in A few moments so no more this time.

This from your Son
Ira

Dear Parents

I recived A letter from you the 15th but have not had time to answer it till today. I went to Nashville the 11th and did not get back till the 15th. I went up with some prisoners and I saw some of our boys that was there in the hospitals. I saw Hiram Bullock. he is in the invalid Corp. and when I got back the boys was moveing their tents so I could not write that day and yesterday I was on guard and came off this morning at half past ten. and I have not got much time to write now. tell Catherine that I will write to her just as soon as we get a little more time. I have not got the Magazine that grandmother sent yet. I got the socks some time ago. but I have not heard from the last ten dollars that I sent home. but I probably hear from it in the next letter that I get. we have had six new recruits in our company. and Lieutenant Corbitt has been promoted to Captain and takes command of company H. he is a good Officer and only about two years older than I am. last night some Gurrillers made an attack on the railroad and captured one train of empty freight cars and burnt them. this is the straightest news that we have had about it. there has been several different rumers about it. they did not take enny prisoners but they robbed what soldiers and Officers there was on the train. it was done some where between here and Nashville. I have not got time to write much more this time so I will close.

This from your Son
Ira

Stevenson, Ala
March 19th 64

Dear Parents

I recived A letter from you this morning dated the 11th in whitch you said that you recived the money all right. tell Father that he may send the old watch and not get A new one yet. but I dont think that he had better send it yet for there is some talk of our going back to the army of the Potomac unless he should have A chance to send it by some one that was comming to the Regiment. I shall know probably by the time that I write again whether it would be safe to send it or not. if we stay here it will be safe enough to send it by mail or express and if we are going back to the Potomac army we will probably know it before long. I have not got my paper very regular for some time back and the two last ones I have not had at all. the weather is warm and pleasant the most of the time but it turns round very cold by spells. when I was going to Nashville I saw peach trees that was begining to bloom out so that they looked quite white and the grass begins to start some. I have made A mistake and wrote on the wrong page but I will number them so you can find out whitch is whitch.

March 20th 64

I did not have time to finish my letter yesterday for they called for me to guard prisoners to clean the streets and I am on guard again today so I cannot write much this time. I have seen Charley Suttell he is one of the new recruits and is in Co. B. the boys are all well with the exception of two or three that have got hard colds.

Ira

Stevenson Ala
March 23rd /64

Dear Parents

I received A letter from you yesterday but I was on guard so that I did not have time to answer it till today. I have not got the paper that Grandmother sent yet but I got the socks some time ago. we are haveing quite winter weather here now   the snow is about six inches deep and if it had not melted it would have been A foot deep. we had quite A time here yesterday   A snowballing   the Colonel challenged our part of the regiment to come out and snowball with the other part of the regiment   so they all turned out   officers and all   and our part was two much for the others so they called out the 60th and 149th to help them. and when they got through there was A good manny black eyes on both sides. it was A nice fight for there was about 300 men engaged   there was not manny verry badly wounded but there was some prety well bruised. I do not hear enny thing more about our going back to the Potomac army so I think it will be safe to send the watch and if he sends it I would like to have it sent as soon as convenient I would be likely to get it the quickest by mail. I want to have him sent the old one I wrote about in my other letter. I have used white oak bark for the disentary since I have been in the army. but we are not troubled with it much now. the regiment is prety health now some of them got hard colds and I have got A hard cold but it does not amount to much. some of the boys are haveing the mumps but I have had them. Milt Knox   Bob Winner and Johney Thompson are all well at Preasent. I think that if you keep Catherine to weed the garden this summer that your largest crop will be weeds. I have not got much more time to write for I have got my gun to clean and several other little things to do so I will close for this time.

From your Son
Ira

Stevenson Ala.
March 27th 1864

Dear Sister

As I have time to write some today I thought that I would write to you. I am well and hope this will find you all the same three of the boys in our company have got the Mumps and some more of them are beginning to complain of sore jaws and I think Milt Knox is going to have them Sol Darling and John Winner was here day before yesterday and stayed one day and one night with us. they expect to work near Chattanooga Sol agreed to write to me as soon as he could and let me know where they are Tom Swan is at work near where we was encamped in Wauhatchie Valley and is encamped on our old Battlefield. he is here this morning he said that he came up to see the boys and then was A going back. tell Father that I dont get more than half of my papers now and when I do get them they dont get here till some time after the other boys get theirs. so I wish he would have it stoped entirely for it dont pay to have it come in that way. I would like to have the paper well enough but I want it to come when it should. the other boys that take the paper get it nearly A week before I do I have not receved the paper that Grandma sent yet. the weather here now is very warm and pleasent the snow did not last long and the ground is getting about dry again. I have not got enny war news to write you see in the papers that General Grant has command of all of the U.S. Forces and that Smith has command of the Potomac Army. things look now as though this Corps. will be likely to stay where it is this summer at least we hope so I have not much more to write this time so I will close.

From your Brother
Ira.

Stevenson Ala
March 28th /64

Dear Parents

I recived A letter from you this morning dated the 20th and I got my paper this morning I wrote in my last letter to have father stop it for it did not come till after all the others did. but I looked at the Directions and see that my papers is directed to Washington and the others are directed to Nashville. so you need not have it stoped but have it directed to Nashville then I will get it when the others do. I am on guard today so I shall not write much besides I wrote A letter to Catherine yesterday. we are haveing A thunder storm here today. I have not got the paper that gramma sent yet it is lost probably so that I will not get it at all. the rain sprinkles through the tent cloths so that it wets my paper so I shall have to stop writing.

Ira S. Jeffers

Newspapers in camp

Stevenson Ala.
April 3rd 1864

Dear Parents

I receved your letter this morning of the 27th. our boys are getting about over the Mumps   Captain Corbitt is sick now with the fever but he is better now   I have not got the magizine that Grandma sent yet   my Republican has been directed to Washington all the time and that is the reason why I have not got that regular. I shall try and write A letter to Grandfather Scofield tomorrow. I am on guard today and shall have to stop writing now to go on post.

I have just been relived from post so I will try and finish my letter now before I have to go on again   when you write to me again send me A darning needle for I have not got enny. Milt Knox and Bob Winner are both well   Milt is here with me writing to. my health is good and I have been on guard every other day for about six weeks so you see that I am enjoying myself about as well as enny of them. I shall have to stop now or not get my letter in the office in time to go today.

Ira

Stevenson Ala. April 9th/64

Dear Parents
    I have not had A letter from you since one week ago today. I wrote A letter to you last Sunday. day before yesterday we had A sort A show on the flat. there was A horse race and foot race wheelbarrow race and A race in corn sacks and A greased pole for the boys to climb. and A greased pig for the niggers to catch and A rooster fight to wind up with. but it is not often that they have such times for we are on guard nearly every other day and when we come off from guard in the morning we have to drill two hours and then go on dress parade. it is reported now that our corps and the 11th corps has been consaladated and is called the 1st corps but there has not been enny order read to us yet to that effect. our boys that was sick have all got well again. I have not heard from Sol since he left here. Bob Winner and Wilt Knox are both well. I cannot write much more now for I have got to begin to get ready for drill. I will write sooner next time and not wate quite so long for A letter.
                    This from your Son Ira

A break down in camp

1) Stevenson Ala.
April 11th 1864

Dear Parents

I receved your letter yesterday of the 3rd but I did not
have time to answer it till today for I was on guard at Head
Quarters. there is one of our boys from this company home
on A furlough but I did not think to write about it for I did
not expect that you would see him for he lives in Kirkwood
and it would be so far out of his way to come and see you   I
have not heard from Sol since he was here   he said that he
would write to me as soon as he got where he could. the
fellows name from our company is Fountain H. Achart but
it is not likely that you will see him   there is some more of
our regiment home on furlough and it may be that you will
see some of them. John Hanleys has been looking for his
furlough for some time   I saw in the paper this morning
that our Corps and the 17th Corps has been Consoladated
and is now the 1st Army Corps and is commanded by Major
General Hooker and General Slocum is to take command of
the forces at Vicksburg. I do not know whither we will stay
where we are this summer or not   some of the Officers think
that we will and others think that we will have to take the
field again. but this railroad has got to be guarded by some
body and it may be us and it may not. but I am in hopes
that they will let us stay here   they cannot get A better man
to command this post than Col. Ireland. I shall have to stop
writing now to attend roll call and get my dinner.
we are having prety warm weather here now but I expect that
it will be A great deal warmer here where we are now than
it was where we was last summer. Milt Knox Bob Winner
and Johney Thompson are all well and I am well. I was glad

to hear that Albert was getting along so well with the Measels and I hope that he will not get enny worse than he has been. I shall have to stop writing now to go on drill it is not likely that I shall have A chance to write enny more in this letter today.

From Ira S. Jeffers

Stevenson Ala.
April 14th 1864

Dear Parents

I wrote A letter to you the 11th but as I got my watch I though that I would write and let you know that it was all right. Major Eldrage brought it to me   he arrived this morning   we was reviewed here today by General Slocum he is our commander no longer. we was sorry to have to part with him and he was sorry to have to leave his old Corps. we are commanded by General Joe Hooker   he is A good General and is well liked by the men   we have consoldated with the 11th Corps and are known as the 1st Army Corps. I wrote to you sometime ago about it in my last letter but I did not know it for certain then   we had the order read to us this afternoon on dress parade. I suppose that we will have to lose the white star now whitch has been so dearly earned but we may be allowed to keep it even if there is a badge got up for the First Corps.   we may be allowed to wear them both   I dont think it would be enny thing more than right the bugle has just sounded for roll call so I shall have to stop A short time.

We have heard cannonading this afternoon down the river quite sharp but have not heard what it was for yet but we expect that General Geary has had A twist with the Rebels. he went down that way the other day with about 3,000 men and two gun boats. I shall know probably when I write again what it was about   I have been to Spelling school this evening and spelt them all down. then they had to try several of the hardest words in the book before they could stick me. I think it is A good way to pass off the evenings and is quite instructive and learn as much as I would playing cards. Bob Winner is well   Milt Knox was here yesterday and said that his jaws was getting sore and he thought that he was getting the Mumps. he is well other ways   I have not seen him today   one of the boys in the regiment that was wounded has got his Discharge and is going home today. I would have my likeness taken and send by him but he has got all that he can carry for the boys in his own company   I have finished my sheet so I will stop.

This from your Son
Ira.

I have been offered 14 dollars for my watch since I got it.

April 19th 1864

Dear Parents

I receved your letter yesterday of the 10th but did not have time to answer it till today for I was on Head Quarters guard. I receved my watch all right I wrote A letter to you the same day that I got it there is A man in Co. "A" of this regiment by the name of Robinson and the boys call him Yankee Robinson but he is not the one that you knew he is at home on A furlough now he lives at Montrose Pa. he is the one that Jim met. we have been consoladated with the 11th Corps and are the First Army Corps. but you need not change the directions on my letters yet tell Grandma that the socks was just A fit and suit me just as well as though they had new tops on for the tops will wear longer than the feet now. and I have A pleanty to eat we draw good new bread every day from the bakery we have A government Bakery of our own and we draw beans Desacated potatoes and we have drawn raw potatoes A few times. besides Pork and some of the time Beef and sugar and coffee. I have been on dress parade since I commenced my letter and there was an order read to us stating that we are to be called the 20th Army Corps. so I suppose that the last must be right I am in hopes that we will stay here this summer for it is A prety good place and we have got things fixed up prety good. they are having A log school house built for the niggers. there is A good many of them here and they are anxious to learn to read there is A few that have got A prety good education but the most of them are ignorant enough but the school house is intended for the little nigs. I suppose for the others are to busy at work to study much. Bob Winner is well Milt Knox has got the Mumps but is about over them now. he did not have them very bad   they only swelled up on one side of his face. I am well but I dont know how black I am for the others are the same color. I suppose that we are A shade or two blacker than the white folks up north. I dont know but we feel just as well. I have got my sheet full so I will stop.

           This from your Son

           Ira.

Stevenson Ala.
April 23th 1864

Dear Parents

I receved your letter this morning of the 12th. I was the only one in our company that got enny   the darning needle came all right and so did the watch   we are having pleasant weather here now and it is getting to be about as warm as I want it to get.   there was A case of Small Pox here amoung the niggers   there tents are only ten rods from ours but I dont think that it has spread enny   there has not been more cases of it as of yet and I hope there wont be   there has been cases of it here before this spring. John Dorman has got back   he said that he seen Father when he was home and Grandfather. he will be likely to get his discharge before long   we are the 20th Army corps now and Colonel Ireland has been assigned to command of this Brigade.   our Lt. Col. VanVarish is to command the Regiment. General Hooker has command of the Corps. I have not got much to write today for I am on guard and have got to hurry up besides the boys are all of the time talking to me. Bob Winner is well and Milt Knox is well   he has got over the Mumps. I will not write enny more this time.

This from your Son
Ira S. Jeffers

April 26th 1864

Dear Parents

I receved your letter this morning of the 17th. I have just came off from guard so I think that I will have time to write some now I have just had my likeness taken and will send it in this letter. it is A good one all except the eyes they look very bad the boys all say that it looks just like me. my coat is wrinkled some but it sets so tight that it would not keep straight. you must make your own comments on it and when you write let me know what your thoughts are about it. and whether it looks enny different from the others I think that it is about time that I got them Photographs that you was to send me some time ago I would like to have them even if I dont get but one at A time. the star on my cap does not show much but you can see A white spot there in my last letter I wrote that the Small Pox had broke out here but there has not been enny more cases of it. they have got nearly all of there corn and cotton planted around here now and those that are able to carry on A Plantation say that they will raise as much this year as they ever did. one Farmer said that he had got 75 acres of cotton and A large amount of corn planted already the woods are leaved out nearly to there full size now. the weather is getting so warm that it is almost uncomfortable I am in hopes that we will stay on this railroad this summer but we dont know what the next two months will bring round. I have not had enny letter from Sol yet if I knew where to direct to him I would write to him. Milt Knox and Bob Winner and myself are all well you can tell by the likeness that the southern climate agrees

with me prety well. I have filled up my paper so I will close
for this time.

From your Son
Ira.

May 1th 1864

Dear Parents
    I thought that I would write A few lines to you today for I do not know when I shall have A chance to write again very soon for we expect to start on A march in A few days but we dont know where we are going. we are ordered to have shoes and clothing for two months and salt for 60 days. from the orders that we are getting I should think that it is likely that we are fitting out for some seperate expedition. the Army at the front is said to be moveing now we have not been relived from this just yet but the troops that are to relive us are nearly all here. one regiment of them are Veterans and have never seen A fight so you can make up your mind that our regiment that have been nearly always always been in the front dont think much of them. it has lead to several knock downs between them the engineers and some of the other men on the railroad say that if this Corps is taken off from the railroad and new troops put on that they shall leave for there is danger enough now they say they want men that know what fighting is. it is reported among the boys that the railroad men have sent in A petition to Washington for to have us stay here but I dont know whether it will work or not. Milt and Bob are well and so am I. I sent my likeness to you in my last letter you will get it probably before you do this one. I will write as often as I can if we march and it is A prety sure thing. write as often as you can.
               From your Son
               Ira.

Near Dalton Ga.
May 10th 1864

Dear Parents

I receved your letter this morning that was mailed the 2nd. it found me well but far from Stevenson we left there the 2nd and have been marching nearly every day since our Brigade has not been in enny of the fighting yet but the rest of the Division has our Brigade went in another direction from the rest of the Division to support Kilpatricks Cavelry and they had A fight just before we got back to them. they drove the Rebs to the mountains and when they got there they had strong entrechments to much for our men at present we worked last night building Breastworks and some of the men are at work yet. we have had some good news from the Potomac Army and I am in hopes that you will soon hear good news from this Army. Milt Knox and Bob Winner are both well. I will not write enny more now but I will try and write again soon. write as often as you can connvintly. they will get to me at times if we dont get our mail every day.

This from your Son
Ira.

In the Field near Castle Ga.
May 20th 1864

Dear Sister

I receved your letter of the 5th last night I was glad to hear from you. It is not often that we get the mail so I look for A letter every time that it does come   I do not get A chance to write very often and we cannot send letters as often as we get them. there has been I think 11 days that there has been fighting here every day   we have not been engaged but one day   our company has not had but one man wounded   he was slightly wounded in the forehead. the Rebels retreated night before last and we followed them all day yesterday and our Cavelry was skirmishing with them   as near as I can learn we are about 25 miles south of Dalton. our Colonel was wounded with A piece of shell the 15th but he will be around again in A short time I think. Bob and Milt are well I cant write enny more now for they are getting the letters to send out.

Ira.

In the Field near Castle Ga.
May 20th 1864

Dear Parents

As I have A few moments so that I can I will try and write A few lines. we have been on the move every day but one since we left Stevenson some days ago   we have not went but A short distance. there has been fighting or skirmishing nearly every day   I belive we have not had enny killed and only 4 wounded besides the Colonel. we had one wounded in our company. he was only slightly and has just got back to us. he says that the Colonel will be back to us in A day or two   he was hit in the back with A piece of shell. I helped carry him to the Hospital   I seen Manser Hatch and Danel Hall just before the fight commenced at Snake Creek Gap. they was both well then   there has been some hard fighting here and it is likely that there will be A great deal more before long for we are pushing them on towards Atlanta. it may be A second Vicksburg to take but we have great confidence in our Generals. but I pray to him that is ruler over all of guidence and protection. he is the General that we should all put the most confidence in   I receved the letter that Father directed to the First Corps but it was detained in Nashville for nonpayment of postage   I got my paper this morning if you put the Corps on the letters have it the 20th other wise direct the same. the most of the boys dont have enny Corps on. Bob Winner and Milt Knox are both well and I am well write as often as you can and not wait for me for I dont get much time to write now and I cant send them every day if I could write them   I will not write enny more this time.

From your Son
Ira

PS. Bob says if Father wants enny help to write and let him know and he will change works with him and Uncle Samuel permitting. he thinks that A change of climate at this present time would be better for his health but he would prefer going North.

Near Cassville Ga.
May 21th 1864

Dear Parents

I wrote A letter to you yesterday but as I have time I thought that I would commence another today we did not march enny yesterday and we are in the same place yet. there is A report in camp that we are to stay where we are A day or two and drew clothing extra shoes etc. for A 20 days march to go on some other expedition but we cannot tell much by what we hear for there is nearly all kinds of reports and rumers in camp. some that are true and A good many that are untrue you hear more of the war news than I do. we dont get many papers so we dont know what is going on only right where we are I seen Norman Vance today he is well. Milt Knox and Bob Winner are both well and I am well. the weather is prety warm here now. corn is large enough to hoe we are where we see some prety good gardens and large fields of grain it is ruining A great deal of it the war is. it is distroying large amounts of property I will wait till tomorrow to finish my letter unless they take A notion to move.

Ira S. Jeffers

May 22nd 1864

Dear Parents

I receved your letter this morning of the 11th. I was glad to hear that you was all well we are all well this morning you said that you thought that I looked prety fat in the likeness. I dont look quite so fat now   these marches takes the flesh off from us some. we are to be ready to start again in A day or two   I suppose we have been stopped here to get rested out A little. we get our mail nearly every day now. the cars run nearly to where we are   there was not many bridges for the Rebels to burn and when they did burn one our men had the timber all ready to put it up again. the men are all in hopes that this campaign will end the war. it looks favorable now but it will cost the lives of A good many men yet but it is in A good cause and God grant that those that fall may be prepared. my Father in mercy improves and instructs me by sorrow and smart vestal by correction removes and shows me the ground of my heart. when you write direct to the 3rd Brigade 2nd Division 20th Corps. the directions have not changed only the Corps whitch is the 20th instead of the 12th. write as often as you can   I was the only one that got A letter in our company this morning.

Ira S. Jeffers

Camp of the 137th Regt. in the field
June 2nd 1864

Dear Parents

It has been some time since I have had A chance to write to you and as I think that I will have time now I will try and inprove the opportaity   I am well at present in both body and mind whitch is indeed A great blessing whitch we ought to feel thankful for. Milt Knox is well   Bob Winner has gone to the Hospital he has another attack of the Dierea   he will be likely to be back again soon.   our Corps has been fighting eight days up to yesterday noon then we was relived by another Corps. we have not heard much fireing today they are probably changeing their position   we are said to be within about 35 miles of Atlanta. some of the regiments in our Brigade lost A good many men but we have not lost but A few. I have not heard how many. we did not lose enny in our company. Bob probably would not have left us but we was in entrenchments and had to be lieing down the most of the time for if we stired about much we apt to get hit by the Rebels Sharp Shooters. I will not write much now but will try and write again soon. to lie on the ground long is apt to bring on the Dierea and Bob has almost always had it. you must write as often as you can for I can get letters oftener than I can send them and when you write be sure to send postage Stamps. I shall put the last one on this letter.

From your Son
Ira

Altona Creek Ga.
June 5th 1864

Dear Sister

As I have not got much else to do I will keep on writeing. I cannot think of much to write but still I will try   I do not know when I will be able to send it but I will get it ready for I may not have A chance to write when they get A chance to send the mail. for they dont know sometimes half an hour before hand. Milt Knox and myself are well. Bob has gone to the Hospital   he has got the Dierea so that he is not able to stand the marching if he can stay to the Hospital   A short time he will get recruited up again   we eat A great deal of fresh beef and have Suck poor water that it gives A good many the Dierea. when Mother writes again have her send me about 50 cents worth of stamps because I write A good many times before I get her letters. I can carry them so as to not spoil them   I had to get one of Milts this morning to put on this letter. I would send her money to get them with but I have not got but A little and shall probably need it all before we get our pay again. Col. Ireland has got back again but he is not well enough to take command yet but he will be probably before long. our captain is sick and has gone to the Hospital so we are commanded by A Leutenant from another company at present. I think I will lay aside my letter now and write some more by and by.

Ira S. Jeffers

June 7th 1864

Dear Sister

We left our camp at the creek yesterday about 10 o'clock to join the rest of the Corps. we passed through A small town on the railroad called Ackworth   came up to the rest of the Division about dark   every thing is quite so far this morning. our troops are changeing there position but I dont know where they are going to nor where we are but as near as I can find out we are about 12 miles from Marietta Ga. it is south of us and to our left   it has been very wet and rainey for about A week back but it has been very warm   nights when it dont rain we spread some leaves on the ground and spread A rubber blanket over them to lie on then we have two cloths and another rubber to put over us. we dont sleep with enny thing over us much of the time. Milt and I tent alone now that Bob is gone. the Regiment got A mail last night but I did not get enny thing   it has been A little over A week since we had enny mail till last night. our Captain got back last night. Milt Knox is well and I am well except my feet are prety sore and blistered by Marching. I commenced to write to Mother on another sheet before I commenced this one but I got the days mixed up so that I will not send it. it was A sort of A diary of the days about what we was doing. I may get A letter before I have A chance to send this and it may be that there will be A chance to send letters before the mail comes in again. no more at present.

This from your Brother
Ira

Dear Parents

I receved your letter this afternoon and lose no time in answering it   I was glad to hear that you was all well. I went back to the Wagon Train this forenoon and saw Bob Winner   he was sent to the regiment when we moved. but our regimental Doctor saw him and told him to stay with the wagons where he could get his things carried A spell yet   he wanted that I should write so that his folks would know how he was for he could not send A letter very well from the train. he is comming back to the company in A few days. the Directions on my letters do not want to be changed   nothing but the Corps whitch is the 20th instead of the 12th. we are in Gearys Division   the 2nd Division. the same as before and the 3rd Brigade. we wear the White Star and will wear it till we die. it will be worn by the soldiers that it belongs to after there return home. it is considered as A Badge of Honor by them. and that no man has A right to take it from them and I pray to God that its Brightness may never be dimed by disgrace. may it never shine less Bright over the Brave Boys that have fallen under it than it does today. may the Lord strengthen us in time of need to protect it. and like the Star of the east guide us to our Saviour Jesus Christ. I have not time to write more for the mail is going out.

Ira.

Camp of the 137th N.Y.S.V.

June 9th 1864

Dear Parents

I receved your letter this morning of the 29th and was glad to hear that you was all well. I wrote A letter to you day before yesterday and receved one from you the same day but I had not sealed up my letter so I wrote you more in it I got A letter from Afrelia Collins yesterday and answered it and this morning I receved your letter of the 29th and two books. I think that I shall send home one of them today and send the other as soon as I get through reading it and I want to have you keep them for me and read them. they cost me One Dollar A year and 25 cents of postage. we was ordered to strike tents this morning for to move but we soon had orders to put them up again that we are not going till tomorrow. so I and Milt put ours up and commenced to write then. we had to take them down again and put them up in regular order but I think now that we can have A chance to finish our letters. I seen Manser Hatch and Danna Hall yesterday and saw Bob Winner. he said that he was A good deal better. I get my paper pretty regular now that is when we get our mails. I have not got the last one yet. the Ordily got his but mine has not come yet. we are about 4 or 5 miles from the railroad and they say that the cars run right through to us. it dont take long for them to fix up the road for it is A prety level country so there is not many bridges for the Rebels to burn. I suppose things look A great deal different here than they do up north. Wheat and Oats are headed out and have been for some time and I have seen corn that was knee high with out straighten it up and the Cherrys are getting ripe. I

will not write enny more now for they think that we cannot
send it today.

Ira S. Jeffers

Camp of the 137th Regt. N.Y.S.V.
June 14th 1864

Dear Parents

Our officers have just told us that we can send letters this afternoon so I will try and write A few lines to you to let you know that I am well. we moved about two miles yesterday from where we was when I wrote to you the last time. we had breastworks there where we was but we have advanced our lines and have built more breastworks. they have been skirmishing here for several days but there has not been enny fighting right here to amount to much   it is reported here today that there was A Corps on our left that took 15 hundred prisoners and one Battery yesterday. the Rebels are fortifying on A hill in front of us but I dont think that our Generals will try to take it from the front. our men have been shelling the Rebels this afternoon but they did not reply to it at all. I get my paper prety regular and the war news in it is about as late as enny that we get. I sent you one of my books that I take now. you will be likely to get it before you do this letter. the last paper that we had said that A. Lincoln was nomanated for the Presidency again and I have not heard who is to run against him. I suppose that the soldiers will have A chance to vote this fall and if they do I shall be old enough to vote for the President and I think that Abraham Lincoln will be the man that I shall vote for. I have not seen Bob since I wrote to you before. Milt Knox and myself are well. we have two recruits in our company from Port Crane. John Randel and West Randel. they are Keefe Randels boys. I dont know whether you know them or not. I think Father knows them they are both well and are both good soldiers. I cannot think of enny thing more to write that will be interesting to you so I will close for this time.

This from your Son
Ira S. Jeffers

Near Marietta Ga.
June 20th 1864

Dear Parents

I receved your letter the 18th but have not much of A chance to write since. Milt Knox and my self are well I have not heard from Bob Winner lately only that he is with the train yet. the Rebels keep falling back from one line to another we keep after them. we get as close to there breastworks as we can at night and build breastworks while it is dark. our Regt. has lost about 25 in killed and wounded. we have had 4 wounded in our Company there names are William J. Smith Foot serious Thomas Foaly Thigh serious Edwin Wright Hand slight Henry Tapping Arm Amputated. we are within about two or three miles of Marietta now. tell Catherine that I want that she should keep all the letters that she sees in the papers from this Regiment. for there is A good many of them from this Company they are in the Standard and Republican. I will not write enny more at present for I dont know whether I can send it this afternoon or not. the Chaplin has just passed by and says he will take our letters about 5 o'clock but I have no more to write now in particular so I will not commence on another sheet. this was A piece.

This from your Son
Ira S. Jeffers

Near Marietta Ga.
June 24th 1864

Dear Parents

I will try and write A few lines to you to let you know that I am well. we are in breastworks as usual we build breastworks first and sleep afterwards that is if we can get A chance we have drove the Rebs about one half mile since I wrote to you the 19th. we keep closeing in on them slowly. there is heavy skirmishing in front of us nearly all of the time our regiment was out on skirmish one day and part of another and one night before we was relived. we had one man killed and 5 wounded while we was out in the Regiment but we did not have enny hurt in our Company. I got my paper yesterday of the 15th our papers and letters are about all the news that we get. we dont get many papers only what come from home but dont we all look for A letter when the mail comes in but we are disapointed many times when we think that we should get them if our folks at home could see what times we have to take to write they would think that they could write every day as easy as we can write once A week but I think that I get letters from home as often as enny of them. some of the time I do not get A chance to write or send them if they was writen but you must not wait to get A letter from me every time before you write. Charley Suttell is well I did not think that he could stand soldiering A great while for he did not look enny to healthy when he first came here but he looks as tough as A bear now. I think that he looks better than he did at home. the Randell boys are both well and Johney Thompson is well. Milt Knox and myself are both well. I do not think of enny more of the boys you know only Bob and I have not heard from him very lately but if he had been enny worse I should have heard of it. Elisha Burgdorf is well   I saw him yesterday   he is in the Pioneer Corps.   I will not write enny more this time for I want to clean my gun.

This from your Son
Ira

Near Marietta Ga.
June 28th 1864

Dear Parents

I receved your letter this morning of the 16th and was glad to hear that you was all well. I am well Milt Knox is well. there is not many sick as I should think there would be in such A campaign as this is. we have been up night and day both some of the time It has been 58 days I think since we left Stevenson but the men stand it well. the weather is very hot here now but I expect that it will be A great deal hotter next month we advanced our line again yesterday about one half mile and built breastworks again. we have built breastworks 13 times so some of the boys said this morning since we started this campaign. our skirmishers and the Rebs had quite A time the other night. they was close enough together so that they could talk to one another so they agreed that they would not fire on one another that night. they said that they belonged to the 76th Kentuckey and the 75th Alabamma Regiments. they was Blackguarding with our boys all night one of our boys asked them if they loved there Country and they said of course they did. then they asked them what they run off and left it for. it looks hard for men to be talking and laughing together and the next moment trying to kill each other the Bullets keep comeing over here from the skirmish line and the Artillery keeps shelling each other there shells are thrown over us from both sides but they have not done much harm to our Regiment yet. there was one man wounded in the next Company to us yesterday with A piece of shell but it was nothing but A flesh wound. we have not had but 4 wounded in our company. I wrote to you about them before we had 40 men come back to the

Regiment yesterday that has been taken prisoners and been to the Hospitals. we stacked 209 guns before they came back we have about 250 men in the Regiment now bearing arms. I cannot write much news to you this time every thing is about the same as it was   you get the most of the war news before we do. write as often as you can conniently and I will try and do the same.

This from your Son
Ira S. Jeffers

Camp of the 137th N.Y.
July 8th 1864

Dear Parents

It has been some time since I have wrote A letter to you but I will try and do so now. we are in camp now where we expect to stay 4 or 5 days till we can wash up some. I say we are in camp but we are in line just the same as we have been but our line is A little farther from the Rebel works than they generaly are. our Regiment is mostly all on picket now they will be relived probably tonight. we are near enough to Atlanta so that we can see it by climbing up trees around our camp it is nearly level from here to Atlanta and it looks as though it was about 8 or 10 miles from here to it. it is A wilderness nearly all of the way to it it is on A rise of ground and is quite A large place. I think that we are about as near to Atlanta as Grant is to Richmond. the weather is very hot here now I think it is as hot here now as I ever see it in Virginia. Bob Winner is here with us now he is well. Milt Knox is well and I am well our company has sent 9 men back to the Hospital sick. I belive since we started on this campaign we had 4 wounded but so far thank God I have been blessed with good health.

To Mother

When you write again write what you was doing the 4th of July. you probably spent your 4th at home where you generaly do. but where ever you was you probably was thinking A good deal of the time about where your boy was and what he was doing. I will tell you. he was thinking of his Mother and what she said to him just before he left home. you said to me that you had rather hear that I was A praying boy than to hear that I kept evil company and was in the habit of getting drunk etc. there was plenty of Whiskey to be had that day but I did not have enny desire to touch enny of it. and the company that I kept consisted of some Religious men and in the evening some 8 or 10 of us got together and had A Prayer Meeting and I feel that I enjoyed my self as well in that way as I could in enny other. when I left home I was young and was thrown among men of every kind. and the greater part of the young men that came to the war have learnt more in the ways of wickedness than enny other. but with the grace of God assisting me if I am ever permitted to return home it may be with such A Name that they will not be ashamed to own me as their son.

Ira S. Jeffers

Camp of the 137th N.Y.S.V.
July 12th 1864

Dear Sister

It has been some time since I have receved A letter from home but I look for one as soon as the mail comes in again. I wrote one letter to Mother since we have been here we are within about two miles of the Chattahoochee River in camp the Rebels are said to be all acrossed the river on the other side and that our pickets are on the bank of the river. the army is not moveing much here at present I have heard that one of our Corps crossed the river yesterday and came back again and have gone into camp but I dont know how true it is. it looks as though we was going to lay still A short time but it is not likely that we will lay still long. some of the boys think that we will have to go back to the Potomac Army if the Rebels get into Pennsylvania again but there is something to be done here yet. we are in sight of it but it may take A good while to get that few miles after all. but when Sherman makes A move on it I think he will be successful. it is very hot weather here now and would be very hard to march A great ways at A time. Bob Winner and Milt Knox are well. John Randell is sick and has been sent back to the Hospital. William J. Smith is reported to be dead but I dont know for certain that it is so he was wounded in the foot he was not thought to be in enny danger when we heard from him last but the Chattanooga Gazette states that he died in the Hospital at that place. I have not seen the paper myself I will know probably when I write again more about it. we did not expect to hear such news about him for we all thought he would get well. I am well at present and hope when this reaches you that it will find you all well. I want you to write

as often as you can   it has been some time since I have had A
letter.   there is times when I do not get A chance to write so
you must not wait for A letter every time before you write.
when I can I shall write often   I have got to stop writeing
now to help clean up the streets.   I shall have to send this
without A stamp this time.

This from your Brother
Ira

July 12th 1864

Dear Parents

I receved your welcome letter this morning of the 26th. I had just writen one to Catherine but had not sealed it up yet I receved the stamps all right and also the Photograph. I was glad that Grandmother sent it to me I have got Grandfathers yet and it looks about as clean as it did when I got it. I dont think that Grandma looks enny different than she did when I went away. the boys all think that it is A nice picture and them that know her say that she dont look enny older than she did 20 years ago. I lost my silk hankerchief the other day but it was getting prety well worn it was not worth much when I lost it. I think I kept it prety well I have wrote A letter this morning to Aunt Malvina. I think I have not had but one letter from her since I have been in the Army and I have writen 4 or 5 to her it may be that she has not receved them. I dont think that she would neglect answering all of them if she had receved all of them I directed my letter to Hornelsville Steuben Co. New York and told her how to direct to me. If I did not direct right when you write again let me know.

I had to stop writeing to get my dinner and now I will try and finish my letter. when you write again you need not send me enny paper only what you write on you can send A package of 24 sheets of paper and as many envelopes for 8 cents. you can send unsealed packages to me for 2 cents for every 4 ounces the other boys have there paper and envelopes come in that way and I wish you would send me A package. put good stout paper around it and tie it well and I dont think there will be enny danger but what it will get here all right then you can write longer letters   tell

Grandfather that there is A Henry Harper in this Regiment but I dont know whether he is the one he means or not   he is from Union. I think he is Commissasire Seargant in this Regiment. Mother I have got A old paper here that I picked up in camp that I am going to send to you   it is as good to me as new   it is the American Messenger. I have subseribed for them and expect to get them soon and I will send them to you when I have read them. and I pray that you may look serious upon what you read in them   and what ever you feel it is your duty to do that and may God help you.

Ira

Camp of the 137th Regt.
Near the Chattahoochee River Ga.
July 15th 1864

Dear Parents

As I have time to write today I will do so although it has not been but A few days since I wrote to you. we are in camp yet   the Rebels pickets are on one side of the river and ours on the other   they are within speaking distance of each other. Bob Winner and Milt Knox are well and I am well   I told Bob that his folks said he did not write very often and that it had been some time since they had A letter from him. he said that some day he would sit down and write A half A dozen and see then if he wrote enough.   he says he cannot think of enny thing to write oftenner that once A month then all that he can think of is to write that he is well and he says that I can write that so that his folks will know that he is well.   he says he would write oftenner if he had enny thing to write   it is A hard matter for some to write if they have ever so much time.   I have writen A good many letters but I dont seem to get enny answers to them only what I write home   I shall wait now till I get A answer from them before I write to them again.   I like to get letters often.   let them come from who they may   I have never receved enny letters from Cousins in the West that you said was A going to write to me   it may be that they have wrote to me and I have not got them.   when you write again let me know where to direct to them and what their names is.   so if I have time that I can write to them   I had rather get A letter than A newspaper. my paper comes prety regular yet   the last one that I have had was dated the 6th   I seen Danna Hall and Manser Hatch the other day   they was both well   Johney Thompson is well   I have not writen much that will be interesting in this letter but as I wanted to write to someone I thought that I would write home. if you send me A package of paper and envelopes send about two quilts and dont put more than 8 cents postage. write often as you can.

This from your Son
Ira S. Jeffers

1) In the Breastworks near Atlanta
July 25th 1864

Dear Parents

It has been some time since I wrote to you and I have receved one letter from you since I wrote. so I will try and answer it   we are now near enough to Atlanta so that we can shell it. the Rebels have got prety strong works here   they can shell us from there works   they have not hit our works but once yet   there was one solid shot hit it but did not do enny hurt. the shell burst all around us but they have not hit enny one yet   we have been in A fight since I wrote to you we had one man killed and three wounded in our Company. I went back to the Hospital with A wounded man from our Company and was detailed by the doctors to stay there that night as nurse for the wounded was comming in so fast that they could not take care of them all with what help they did have. so I was not in all of the fight   I cannot write much this time for I am on detail to go and build Breastworks further in front so as to work up as close to the Rebels works as we can. we have got to work up to their works by degrees now. I receved 4 stamps in the last letter that I got from you and I receved Grandmothers Photograph some time ago   if I have time I will send another book with this letter   I will put A stamp on this one. I did not put enny on the others but they should have went through just the same. I have sent two or three of them books and one paper. Bob Winner and Milt Knox are both well. Johney Thompson is well and I am well I would like to write A longer letter if I had time.

From your Son
Ira

Near Atlanta Ga.
July 31th 1864

Dear Parents

I receved your letter of the 17th 3 or 4 days ago but I had just wrote A letter to you. I do not have much of A chance to write here about these times   we are near enough to Atlanta so that we can shell it   when I wrote to you before I was just going on fatigue duty to build Breastworks. we have been in them some time   they have commenced A kind of siege here now I should think. General Hooker has been relived of command at his own request and General Williams is in command of the Corps. the boys all hate to have him leave us   they think as much of him as they do of Sherman. from what I hear I guess that the Western Generals and Eastern Generals can not agree enny better together than the Eastern and Western men but the men agree better than they used to. it is very hot weather here now but for all that we have to work some times prety hard building Breastworks etc. Milt Knox and Bob Winner   Johney Thompson and myself are all well at present. I cannot write enny war news this time as I know of none more than what you get in your paper. we dont get much war news till we get our papers from Binghamton. I get my paper as regular as I could expect and the other boys get the Standard   I have sent for another paper but it has not come yet   it is A Reglious paper called the American Messenger. I cannot think of much to write this morning but I thought that I would write enough to let you know that I am well.

Ira S. Jeffers

Near Atlanta Ga.
August 1st 1864

Dear Parents

I receved your letter of the 24th just now and will try and answer it before dark your letter found me enjoying good health us usual. Bob and Milt are well we are about one mile and A half from Atlanta we are near enough so that our Batteries can shell it and they are doing it this afternoon. they commenced throwing shells about an hour ago and have kept it up prety lively ever since. the Rebels throw some back in return some of our Batteries are throwing at the Rebels Forts. they have got three forts just in front of us we have got good breastworks they are made to stand shell or shot they are dug down into the ground about 4 feet and the dirt is thrown up in front. it has been reported in the papers that we have taken Atlanta but we have not and it looks as though it might be some time yet before we get it. but I dont think that there will be much left of it if our men continue to shell it whitch they will be likely to unless they give up. we have got it about half or two thirds surrounded but there is A chance for them to get out yet. you need not send that package of paper I have bought some so that with what you send me I can get along for sometime. you send me enough only when I write to someone else then I do get short. I do not write many letters only to you the most of my other letters I write to Afrelia Collins. Bob got his letter when I got mine I shall have to stop writeing now to help the other boys get our supper. there is 4 of us that mess together and tent together so we all have A hand in the cooking.

Now I have been to supper I will try and finish my letter. Mother I am glad to hear that you have sought the aid and protection of our Father in Heaven. he will be true to us if we but seek his face and call upon him in spirit and in truth. oh Mother pray to God and ask him to give us Grace and strenght to overcome every evil and sin that doth so easily beat us and turn us from the sins of this World. we are but poor wicked creatures at the best but God will be merciful unto us and save us if we but call Him. it is getting dark and I shall have to stop writeing now.

Ira

August 2nd 1864

As the mail will not go out for sometime yet I will try and write some more. Catherine wrote that Charley Sottelle was dead   I had not heard of it before so I went to the Company and asked them   they said that he had been sent to the Hospital sick and they had not heard from him since till last night.   one of the boys had A letter from some one at Binghamton   they wrote that he was dead but the company has not had enny notice of his death   you wanted to know if I have been to Marrietta. I have not been there for our Corps did not go thought there. but it is said to be A very prety place   it is on the railroad and is where we get our supplys   they are bought as far as there on the cars and then they are drawn in wagons the rest of the way. we are haveing enough to eat at present   we have plenty of rations on this campaign but now that General Joe has left us we may not get as much. some of the other corps on this campaign have been A bit short of rations   when we have had A plently   it is begining to rain so I shall have to finish my letter in the tent. we have had considerable rain for A few days so that the air feels some cooler than it did   it is pretty hot here the most of the time. I cannot think of enny thing more to write so I will close. write as often as you can and I will try and write often remember me in your prayers and may God help us and give us Grace that we may serve him acceptabaly that we may be permitted to inherit A portion in that heavenly Kingdom.

From your Son

Ira

August 10th 1864

Dear Parents

I thought that I would try and write A few lines to you today to let you know what we are doing and how we are getting along. we are in the same Breastworks that we was when I wrote to you before and are building A fort to put some heavy guns in we can shell Atlanta from here with our light pounder Parrot guns but I suppose they intented these big guns to batter down the forts and other obstructions. our Fort will be within A half A mile of two Rebel forts they have got three of the Big Guns here now and they say that they are going to bring up three more. three Brass ones and three Iron Rifle guns. when we was on picket the other day one of the rebel Deserters came in and he said that some of our Rifle balls went into Atlanta from the picket lines and that A great many of our shell went clear over the city. we can see the city by climbing up into the trees but the woods are so thick that we cannot see it with out it has been reported in the papers that we have had Atlanta for some time. Milt Knox and Bob Winner are both well at present and I am well there is several in the Regiment that is getting the Scurvy but they will be likely to get over it in A short time if they are sent back to the Hospital. it is commenceing to rain so I shall have to stop writeing for the present. it is some time since I have had A letter from home. the mail seems to be prety small that comes to our company. yesterday all that came to the Company was one paper and they was only one letter the day before and the boys begin to find fault about it. some think that there folks dont write and others think that the mail is not tented to as strictly as it should be I think that I get my share of letters when they do come. some of the boys say that they will trade off there pens and writeing materials prety soon for tobacco if there folks dont write before long. write as often as you can and I will try and do the same. so no more for this time.

Ira

Dear Sister

I will try and write A few lines to you today. I wrote A letter to Mother yesterday and the big guns that I wrote about they have got into position and fired them all night last night and are fireing them yet today. they fired three shots in five minutes all night you may think that we did not sleep much but we have got used to such noises our pickets keep A fireing night and day I was on picket last Sunday and came off A Monday. the Rebels fired some shots pretty close to us but we did not have enny one hurt in our Regiment our Regiment goes on picket every 6th day there is 6 Regiments in the Brigade and each one takes its turn on picket. it has not been very pleasent doing picket duty for it has rained nearly every day for some time the Rebs keep deserting and comeing in to our lines and they say that there is A good many more that would come in if we did not fire so much so that they could have A chance to. when you write to me again write where to direct to Uncle Toms Children. I would like to write to them so as to hear from them occasionly I think that I wrote to you once before to send me the directions but you must of forgotten to write me the directions I do not get enny letters from enny one but Afrelia and from home. Uncle Lew and Uncle George and Wallace have ceased to write entirely but I wrote to them last so they can not blame me if I do not write to them I like to get letters and I like to write when I can have time to. Bob Winner and Milt Knox are well and I am well there is A good many of the boys in the regiment getting the Scurvy otherwise the health of the Regiment is pretty good. I look for A letter today when the mail comes in but I shall have to put this in the office now for the letters go out before the mail comes in. but I will answer your letters as soon as I can after I get it.

This from your Brother
Ira

Near Atlanta Ga.
August 16th 1864

Dear Parents

I receved your letter of the 7th last evening and will try and answer it now. we have had inspection this morning or I should have commenced my writeing earlyer. I receved Grandfathers letter and photograph all right and answered it as soon as I could and I receved A letter from Aunt Malvina the 12th she said that I must not get angrey for she had answered all of the letters that she had receved from me. she said that she had not heard from you in some time. she wrote that her health was very poor this summer and that she has to keep A hired girl to help her do her work. Theodore is Conducter on the railroad we are in the same place that we was when I wrote to you before and every thing is about the same. I went on picket A Saturday and came off A Sunday our boys made an agreement with the rebs A Sunday not to fire on one another so it was quite peaceable to what it is as A general thing. Milt Knox and Bob Winner are and I am well I have sold my watch it got out of repair in A short time after it got back. I got 8 dollars and A half for it it was getting so that it cost more to keep it in repair than it was worth I got two dollars now and the rest payday but I dont know when we shall be paid again we have not been paid enny on this year yet so when we do get it there will be quite A little pile of it. we are to have 16 dollars A month from the 1st of May Corperels 18 dollars and Seargents 20. I have got another book and A paper that I think that I will send you in A few days I got my paper last evening that I told you that I had subseribed for I will try and send it to you in A few days   it is begining to rain so I shall have to put up my writeing. so no more at present.

                                This from your Son
                                Ira

Near Atlanta Ga.
August 23th 1864

Dear Parents

It has been about A week since I have receved A letter
from you and since I have wrote to you so I will try and
write A few lines to you today. I sent A book and A paper
to you yesterday   they was both done up together. I did
not have enny two cent stamps so I sent it without A stamp
Norman Vance was here day before yesterday to see me   he
said when I wrote to you again to send his best respects to
you and Father. he has got to be Second Leutenant now   he
used to work at Williams Ogdens and Stub Friers. we have
been haveing considerable amount of rain for A spell but
it has cleared off now and is prety hot again today. we are
laying in the same breastworks that we was when I wrote
to you before. I do not know of enny war news to write to
you   there is some talk that we are to be consoladated with
another Regiment and I should not be much surprized if we
was and that before long to. so one of the two Regiments
will have to lose its number   we will have to be consoldated
before long or be filled up with recuits. Milt Knox and Bob
Winner are well. tell Grandmother that Elisha Burgdorf is
sick and has been sent to the Hospital   he has been in the
Pioneer Corps for about A year so that he has not been with
the Company much. I shall hear from him probably before
long if he did not go farther than the Division Hospital but
if he was sent to Chattanooga or Nashville I will not be likely
to hear from him. the mail has just come in and I receved A
letter from you and Uncle George. you wrote that you did
not want that I should reenlist. I do not think that I shall
it is not my intentions now at least I do not think there is

many in the Regiment that would reenlist if they had the chance for we have seen A great deal of hard service but I have enlisted in the service of the Lord and pray that I may serve him faithfully as A true soldier of Jesus Christ.

Ira

Dear Mother

I feel today that I must try and write A few lines to you concerning my Spiritual welfair and Religious experince. about the commencment of this campaign I felt strangely and deeply convicted of my sinfulness and wickness   I felt that I was not makeing the proper use of Gods time.   the time that he has given to all of us poor creatures here below to make our peace with him   to make our choice to dwell in that heavenly land or be cast off for ever   we should inprove that time while we can for we know not at what time we shall be called before our maker and the judgement seat of God. I feel to praise and bless his holy name for turning me from the downward road to distruction.   to the Lord he will save you if you call upon him trusting in him beliveing that he is able to save you.   He has said in his blessed word "All things what so ever ye shall ask in prayer beliveing ya shall receve" Matt 21th 22.   read the General Epistle of James and make the bible your constant companion and guide.   I would like to write more but they are makeing so much noise that I cannot write what I would like to.

Ira

Near Atlanta Ga.
August 25th 1864

Dear Sister

I receved your letter last night dated the 14th and mailed the 16th. I receved A letter from Mother and Uncle George day before yesterday   while she was at Whitneys Point and answered them yesterday   so I shall not have much news to write today. Danna Hall was here yesterday   he said that Manser Hatch has been wounded   he was hit in the arm with A musket ball. it hit the bone and the Doctor took out A piece of the bone but he said that he would not have to lose his arm. he told Danna to write to his folks how he was so that they might know why he did not write. I wrote to Mother that there was some talk of consoldateding us with another Regiment but they say now that they are not going to consoldate enny more so we will probably be filled up with recruites and I had just as live haveing the Regiment filled up by recruits for then we will keep our number and our Officers the same as we are now but if we was consoladated one Regiment would lose its number and the Commisitioned Officers in one of the Regiments would have to be mustered out. I want that you should have your Photograph taken and sent to me for I would like to see how you all look. I have had mine taken twice since I have been down South and sent them home to you and now I think I had ought to have yours   I shall have to hurry up my letter to have it go out in the mail this morning. Milton Knox and Robert Winner are well and I am well. write as often as you can and I will try next time to fill out A whole sheet but I have not got time now.

This from your Brother
Ira.

Camp of the 137thm N.Y.S.V.
On the Chattahoochee River
August 29 1864

Dear Parents
　I receved your letter this evening dated the 27th after I came off from picket. we are now camped on the bank of the Chattahoochee River　we are on the south side　we marched back to here in the night arrived here at day light of the 26th we was not forced to fall back but was ordered here to cover the railroad while the rest of the army made some move at another point. we are building Breastworks now　I have got to write my letter tonight by candle light for I expect to be on detail on the Breastworks in the morning so that I shall not have time to write then. Bob Winner is not very well at present　he has got the Diereah. Milt Knox and myself are well　I wrote to Catherine about Manser being wounded as soon as I heard of it　he was wounded in the arm and had A piece of bone taken out but Danna said that the Doctor said that he would not lose the arm. I receved the letter that you wrote for Grandfather and I wrote A letter to you and one to Grandfather soon after I got it. so you will probably get that letter some time before you will get this and I have sent you another book that you will probably get before you get this letter and there was A paper done up in the last one. I am pleased to hear that you like the books and that the rest of the folks like to read them. Pat Harris has been detailed at Brigade Head Quarters as Postmaster so that he has got A good position for A private soldier. Hank Rummer just went by where I am writeing so he told me to write that he was well. they are drumming now for roll call so I shall have to put up my writeing for A few minutes. I receved the stamps

that you sent all right. I cannot write much more tonight for my candle is getting about burned out and it is getting late.
From your Son
Ira

Dear Parents

I was not on detail this morning on the first call for they did not call as many men as I thought that they would but I shall probably be on in the course of two or three hours. John Hanly is going to write some in my letter   he is one of my best and nearest friends that I have in the Army. he is like an older Brother to me   I will close now.

From your Son
Ira

Write some in my letter to John.

Camp Of The 137th Regt. N.Y.S. Vols.
On The Banks Of The Chattahoochee River
Georgia. August 30th 1864

Mr. Jeffers, Dear Sir.

As Ira was writeing home today I asked the priviledge to write a few lines to you. Although a stranger to you, my name may be familiar, for Ira I presume has mentioned me in his letters he has sent you before this. Ira and myself are intimate friends, not soldiers for our country but soldiers of the Corps and are endevring to fight that good fight of faith. That we may lay hold to eternal life. Some men carry the idea that its impossible to lead a Godly life in the Army but I know by a blessed experience that we can live a Christan life even in the Army notwithstanding the privileges we are deprived of in attending Church and Sabbath schools also the Prayer circle where I was to meet with my friends at home. But Jesus is every where present and will own and bless his people here as well as any place. Necessity compels me to close for this time. If all is well I will write more some other time.

From a Soldiers Friend
Sergt. John Hanly

On picket South of Atlanta Ga.
Sept 5th 1864

Dear Parents

I am on picket today   I wrote A letter to you yesterday but as I have A good chance to write here I thought that I would commence another today. Milt Knox and myself are on post together and are both writeing letters home   It is A great deal of satisfaction to us that we can date our letter at South of Atlanta for it has been some time that we could date them Atlanta. Bob Winner was sent to the Hospital from our camp on the Chattahoochee River and I have not heard from him since for we moved from there in A few days after that so that he was probably sent to Chattanooga but if I chance to hear from him I will write and let you know. he agreed to write to me as soon as he could if he was sent back farther than the Division Hospital   the cars came into Atlanta the next day after we got here and now we can hear the trains come quite often   it will soon be quite A stirring place again. there has been some very hard fighting south of here with the rest of Shermans Army and yesterday the Ambulance trains came in with A good many of the wounded. they brought in A large number of prisoners with them. I have not heard much of the particulars about the fight but they said that our men was successful and routed the Rebs   some think that the campaign is done for the present but I do not know hardly what to think   I think that Sherman has accomplished all that he thought of doing when he started this spring. our Army has been very successful this summer though the guideness and protection of that Divine power whom we should not fail to look to in the hours of success as well as the hours of danger we should render thanks to him for the victorys that we have gained in the several parts of our great Army and may we continue to be successful till this rebellion is brought to A close.

This From your Son

Ira

Atlanta Ga.
September 11th 1864

Dear Parents

It has been some time since I commenced to write this letter but as the railroad has been cut so that we could not receved enny mail so I did not try to finish this and since I commenced to write this letter we have met with A great loss to ourselfs as A regiment and also to our Country by the Death of our much Loved and Honored Officer Colonel David Ireland. he died after an illness of about one week   he was taken with the Chronic Dierea whitch the Physicians was unable to check whitch soon terminated in the Death of him we so muched Loved. he has shared all of our hardships and perils for the two years that we have been in the service of our Country. he was taken from us so suddenly that we can scarcely relize that he is no more to be with us here upon earth. he Died yesterday morning at two o'clock at his Head Quarters. they wanted to take him to the Hospital the day before but he did not want to go   his remains was Embalmed and sent to Binghamton for interment   the Regiment was formed and marched to Brigade Head Quarters by Leutant Colonel VanVoorish to take A farewell look at our old Commander and from there we escorted his remains to the cars where he was left in charge of Chaplin Roberts who is to go north with him. General Geary and Staff also went to the cars with the body. the Colonel was always A great favorite with him but he has fallen not by the bullets but by Disease while serving his country. I wrote to you some time ago that Manser Hatch was wounded   I did not hear from him again until day before yesterday then there was one of his company here and he said that one of the boys in the Company had

A letter from the Hospital stateing that Manser was dead I could not learn enny Paticnlars concerning him so I am unable to give you much information concerning him. Bob Winner has came back from the Hospital he has been unwell but is about well again   Milton Knox is well and I am well. our captain has been unwell for A spell back but he is getting better. the campaign is over for the present   the Army is getting into position to rest and recruit up A little   I expect that our corps will stay here at Atlanta till things commence into campaign. so I am in hopes that we will get paid off soon I think it is about time and I think that we have earned what is due us. I will close for the present   write soon and I will endevor to write often. we receved A mail this afternoon so the railroad probably is all right now.

This from your Son, Ira

Camp of the 137th N.Y.S.V.
Atlanta Ga. Sept 12th 1864

Dear Parents

I will try and write A few lines to you today to let you know that I am well and where I am   we are now in Possession of Atlanta. we started from the Chattahoochee River Sept 2nd in the afternoon and arrived here at Atlanta about two o'clock at night.   there had been A force sent out from the Corps in the morning and learned that the Rebels had evacuated the place before we started   they had to leave for Sherman was comeing around in the rear of them with the rest of the Army. we are on the south side of the city. we came out here yesterday and took up our position on the Augusta Railroad we are in the Fortifications that the Rebels built   they had A strong line of entrenchments extending I should think clear around the city besides several very large Forts. it was very strongly fortified and would have taken A good while to have taken it from the front   it is A very prety city   some very nice buildings in it and from what I have seen of it   it is not as badly knocked to pieces by our shells as I expected. it was but I dont think that I have been in the part where the hardest of the shelling was done. besides the most of it I passed through in the night   there is A great many of the inhabitentes here yet. I suppose there was A good many that could not get there things away so they stayed with them   they had holes dug in the ground to go in when they was shelling. there is A family of the Whitneys liveing here that came from near Binghamton   they are I understand some connection to Ott Whitneys. there is said to be A great many New York State people liveing here   it may be that if we lay here long that I shall find out that I know or that knows some of my folks. I got A couple Rebel papers but there is not much news in them   I dont know but what I will send to you   I dont know whether I wrote to you that General Slocum had Commanded of us or not. he took command of us the last of last month so he has command of his old Corps again   he is A good General and is well liked by his men specially by the Broome County boys for he came out as Colnel of the 27th N.Y.S. Voll. I will not write enny more at present for I do not know when the mail will go out   the railroad is said to be cut between Nashville and Chattanooga so that it may make A difference about sending out our mail. I am going on picket so cannot write enny more.

This from your Son

Ira

Camp of the 137th Regt. N.Y.S.V.
Atlanta Ga. Sept. 13th 1864

Dear Parents

Father I came off from picket this morning and when I got into camp I found two letters here for me from you dated August 28th and September 4th but the Regiment had changed camp while we was out so we had to work fixing up our tents again so that I did not have time to write till this evening. I and Milt are both writeing now Milt is well Bob is with the Company but is not very tough his health quite poor and our Captain is sick and has gone to the Hospital so that we have not got any Commissioned Officers to command the Company at present. we have got 27 men that is with the Company or on detached service within the Division and 22 of them are with the Company we had 98 enlisted me in the Company when we came out and this spring we had 11 recruits added to the Company whitch makes 109 (one hundred and nine) men in all 27 of whitch are left. the rest are sick or wounded or Dead some from wounds receved in Battle others from Disease. some have been put in the Invalid Corps others Discharged or Deserted and of the 11 recruites that we receved this spring there is only 3 (three) left with us. of the recruites one was killed in action and one died from the effects of wounds and one Deserted. the rest are absent sick except the three that are yet with us. I have given you as good A discription of the Company as I can at present I cannot tell now how many men there is in the Regiment at present but I belive that there is but one Company in the Regiment that is larger than ours and there is some that is A great deal smaller. as to President I dont think that McClellan will get as much support from the Army as he will from the people at home I think there is no doubt but what Lincoln will be elected. my vote would not make much different but if I have A chance to cast A vote it will be for Abraham Lincoln. I think it is my duty just as much as it is to fight for my Country I want you to vote this year dont let the Copperheads and Peace men at enny terms rule the comeing election. I am anxious to have the war come to A close but I want that it should be Honorable and I want to see the old Government established and see the Stars and Stripes flowing over every Fort and city from whitch it has been driven by the hands of Cesessions. it is getting late so I shall have to stop for this evening. if I have A chance I will write some more in the morning.

Sept 14th 1864

Dear Parents

I have A short time to write this morning before the mail goes out so I will try and inprove it   I get my Republican as regular as I could expect to on account of the railroad has been cut for some time back so that we could not get enny mail. tell Father to keep up my Subscription for another year   I wrote to you in A letter before this one about the Death of Colonel Ireland. you will probably get it before you do this one so it will be of no use for me to write about it in this letter and I wrote to you that Manser was dead that was what one of his Company told me. I shall have to stop writeing now and go to work cleaning up the street so no more at present.

To Father and Mother
Ira

1) Camp of the 137th N.Y.S.V.
Atlanta Ga. Sept 21th 1864

Dear Parents

I receved your welcome letter of the 12th today but did not have A chance to write till today. I am well at present Bob is quite smart now he is gaining finely Milt is well he went on picket today it has rained very hard nearly all of the afternoon but we have got good board tents built so that we are quite comforable. I am on picket about once in 4 days but when we are in camp they keep us at work fixing up streets and clearing off parade grounds etc most of the time. Captain Milo Eldrage has been mustered as Major he has had his Commission for some time he is A good officer and is well liked by all of the boys. I have writen to you before about the death of Col. Ireland you have probably got the letter before this time. the Brigade is commanded now by Col. Barnum of the 149th N.Y.S.V. Sol and John are quartered here in the city but I cannot get A chance to go and see them for we are kept so busy at present. I expect that Captain Shipman will be here before long with his new company there is A good many boys enlisted in the company that I am acquainted with I have just been looking over my Photographs but I do not see some yet that I would like to send you. I have kept what I have got just as nice as they was when I got them it does me A good deal of good to have them to look at once in A while I think I shall have some Photographs taken to send home and to my friends as soon as we are paid off if I have A chance to. the Bugle is sounding for roll call so I shall have to put up my writeing for tonight. I will try and write some more in the morning before I go out on picket that is if I have time so that I can.

Sept 23 1864

I did not have time to finish my letter yesterday before I went on picket so it had to lay by till today. it rained very hard nearly all of the time that I was out. when we got posted on picket we generally find out what ticket A man will vote for before we leave and I have never been on post yet but what the majority was for Lincoln. I think that McClellan is playing out fast with the Army but still there is some that will vote for him and talk as though that they thought that he would be elected and that he would end the war as soon as he came in power but I cant see it.

This from your Son
Ira

Dear Parents

It has been some little time since I had A letter from you but I will not wate for one for I have A chance to write this afternoon and I may not have as much time again in some time. I came off from picket about noon and the Regiment went on Division drill so I did not have to go for I had but just come off picket. so I have had A quiet time of it just now. we have got our camp fixed up now so they have gone to drilling. they are going to building new forts and breastworks nearer the city than the Rebs had then so that it will not take so many troops to Garrison the place. I expect that Division will have the most of them to build and if they do I hope that we can stay and be the ones to hold them. we do not get much rest here but if I do have as good health as I usually have I shall enjoy the work and drilling about as much as if we was to do nothing. I dont borrow trouble about such things as they come and always to be ready to do my duty when called upon   so that I think that I enjoy myself as well as enny body can in the Army. our mail does not come very regular at present for the Rebs are cutting the railroad every chance that they get but I think that they will get sick of that fun before long. I receved A letter from Aunt Malivina the 27th   she wrote that her folks was well and that she was going to Binghamton in A few days so she has probably been to our house before this time. Bob Winner says that it has been over A month since he has had A letter from home   he says that he thinks his letters must have been miscarried for he thinks that they must have wrote to him   Bob is about the same as he has been for some time   some days he is almost as well as he ever was and the next day he will be down again. Milt and myself are well   I have not seen Sol nor John but once that was when they got here   I cannot see them days for they are to work in the woods but I think that I will go to the Col. and get A pass and go down there some night then I will be likely to find them. tell Father to remember the election this fall. I have just bought A Chattanooga daily paper that I will send him   it is but A small sheet but it sometimes gets in some big things.

Ira

1) Camp of the 137th N.Y.
Atlanta Ga. Oct 16th 1864

Dear Parents

It has been some time since I have writen to you for our commumocations have been cut so that we could not send mail nor get enny so I thought that there was no use of my writeing letters to lie here in the office. Day before yesterday was the first time that mail has come through since the road has been cut. I receved two letters from you the first day mailed the 20th and 26th of Sept and the book that Father sent and two Republican and A letter from Aunt Emiline and one from Fay Hooper so I was prety well stocked with reading the first day and yesterday I got A letter from Afrelia Collins. now if the mail runs all right again and I can get time I will try and write as often as ever they are very busy here building forts and breastworks around the city it keeps us prety busy A part of the First Division and A part of our Division went out on A forageing expedition to get grain for the Mules and horses that was starving to death we went out about 25 miles from Atlanta and found plenty of corn Sweet Potatoes Hogs Sheep etc we soon filled up our wagons with Corn and came back. we was only gone three days and nights and did not meet with much opposition our Cavalry had some little skirmishing with the Rebel Cavalry but not with enny very great force. I think that I wrote to you in my last letter that Bob Winner was sent to the Hospital again I have heard from him once since we got back they said that he was very sick I shall go and see him as soon as I can then I will write to you or his folks how he is and how he is getting along. Milt and myself are well at present. I think that we will get our pay before long for some of the

Regiments have been paid in our Brigade and it must come our turn before long. we will probably get eight months pay tell Father to remember that elections is pretty near at hand and that he must not let the old men stay at home that will vote for Lincoln because they cannot get to town   if he has to hire A team himself to take them there   the old men can do something at election if they are to old to do enny thing in the Army it is A victory worth striving for and every man should do his best. I will write again.

This from your Son
Ira

Dear Parents

I receved two letters yesterday dated the 4th and 12th of Oct   one from you and one that you and Catherine wrote and also two of my papers. tell Father to pay for my paper for the next year when my time is up I want it kept up as long as I am in the service   I have not wrote but two or three letters in A long time for we could not send them if we could. it seems to me as though it has been two months since the Rebels have commenced to tear up the railroad   it is all right again now but how long it will stay so I dont know. there is enough here for us to do we have been busy at something ever since we have been in Atlanta   we have got the fortifications about done. we are now takeing up railroad iron south of Atlanta and sending it on where the rebels have torn up the road between here and Chattanooga. we expect to guard the train down as far as East Point again today after another load   I expect every minute to hear the orders to fall in so I write about as fast as I can. we have been paid off and I have sent 80 dollars by way of the Postmaster you will receve A letter from him with A check in it for the amount on some one of the banks in Binghamton. if you do not just write to me you will not be likely to get it till about A week after you get this letter for I dont think that he has left here yet. I receved the letter that Fay wrote to me   I did not have enny trouble to read it   I shall answer it as soon as I can get time to. I shall try and do it today   when you write again write how to direct to Sarah Sharp so that I can write to her some time when I have time   I am sorry to hear that Grandmother has been so unfortunate as to fall and hurt her self but I am in hopes that she will soon be well again. Bob Winner is gaining some now I have not seen him but some of the other boys have. Milt Knox and myself are well   we tent together yet. we have got us A good board tent built and A good fireplace in it. the weather is quite cool here now some of the time but I suppose it is A great colder up north I shall not write enny more now for I want to send it in this mail. so no more at present.

This from your Son
Ira to his Parents

Camp of the 137th regt NY Vols
Atlanta Ga. Oct 26th/64

Dear Parents

I received A letter from you today it was dated Oct. 16th and will try and answer it this evening. they are getting the Railroad prety near fixed so that we can send letters and get some once in A while it has been so some of the time that we could not get enny letters or send enny for two weeks so when the mail did come the letters was all in A heap but I was glad to get them then. the regiment went out on A forageing expectition today and expect to be gone 5 days I was left in camp for to guard the camp till they get back again so I shall have time to write some before they get back if nothing happens. I answered three letters today and have got two yet to answer I intended to write to you today or tomorrow whether I got A letter from you or not. we have been paid off we got 8 months pay and I put 80 dollars in the Colonels hand to send home by the paymaster and got A receipt for it. when the paymaster gets to Binghamton he will deposit the money in the bank of Binghamton and he will send A check to Leverett Jeffers so that he can draw the money. it may take A little longer to send it in this way but it is A great deal the safest way for the mail is verry uncertain between here and Nashville and at the time I sent in my money there was not much prospects of getting it through by the mail at all. the paymaster has not left here yet. Major Rogers paid us. Bob Winner is quite sick he is in the Hospital I have not had A chance to go and see him yet but I have seen some of the boys that come from there nearly every day they are sending the sick all back to Chattanooga and Nashville it may be that Bob has been sent back. I have not seen enny of the boys from there for the last two days. Norman Vance was here to see me today he inquired about all of my folks and told me when I wrote home to send you all best respects and also to all inquireing friends. he inquired about all of the young People about the neighborhood but as you do not write to me about them I could not give him much information concering them. the Recruits that is comeing to this Regiment have not got here yet but I have heard that they are on their way between here and Chattanooga so they will get here before long I think. tell Catherine that I shall try and write to her in A day or two and tell Grandmother that I do not Forget her if I do not write to her but I was verry sorry to hear that she has been so unfortunate as to fall and hurt her and in hopes that she will soon be well again I shall have to close my letter now for it is time that I went to bed.

This from your Son
Ira S. Jeffers

Atlanta Ga. Nov 1st 1864

Dear Parents

I will try and write A few lines to you to let you know how I am. when I wrote to before the Regiment was out on A foraging expedition they got back all right and brought back their wagons prety well loaded with forage for the teams. I went and seen Bob Winner while they was gone   he is very sick but I think that the worst of his sickness is over I think that if he has enny thing of A chance and dont take cold or enny thing that he will get along first rate. he will be sent back to Nashville as soon as the Hospital cars come up so that they can   when he gets there he will have A good place to stay and such food as he wants. he had a letter from his folks A short time ago. our boys are all well that you know. A part of the Recruits that was comeing to our Regiment have got here   the rest of them are comeing with cattle   we expect them here in A day or two   I have not seen but one of them that I know yet   that is Jim Liskes boy. I have not had much talk with them yet. there is some talk of our moveing but I dont know enny thing about it so I cant write enny thing about it   we may move and we may not. I will write as offen as I can if we do and as soon. I will try and write again soon so that you can know what we are doing. it has been almost A week since I wrote to you but it dont seem as though it had been half of that time   it was reported that there was quite A force of rebels hanging around near here last night. but if we have got to fight them enny more I would like to have them charge on our works here about six or eight lines deep   I think that we could annihilate the rest of Hoods army. but I dont think that they will try that. there was some little fireing on the picket last night but it did not amount to much   just enough to make them vigilant and watchful. I dont think that enny thing serous will come of it still there may   but we hope for the best always and also that the best man for President will be Elected. I started my note to father the 28th I want to know if he got it in time to put it in. tell Grandma that I have not forgotten her if I do not write to her but mean to try and write A letter to her some when I have time.

This from your Son
Ira

Camp of the 137th N.Y. Voll.
Atlanta Ga. Nov 3rd 1864

Dear Sister

I receved your letter today of the 24th with the photograph in it all right. I think that it is good one   you look some older than you did when I went away   I would like to have mine taken but I cannot as things are now. we are drawing clothing and things for A two month campaign. I do not know where we are going nor when but I will try and write often so as to let you know what we are doing. that is if there is enny chance to send letters   it may be that we will not move at all. I was glad to hear that Grandmother is getting well again. Bob Winner has been sent back to Chattanooga or Nashville so I shall not have much more of A chance to hear from him than his folks will. the other boys are well that you know and I am well with the exception of A head ache whitch does not amount to much. we are haveing some wet rainly weather here now   it will be A pretty bad time to start on anouther campaign but it will probably be worse for the recruits than it will be for us   I think that we are as well able to stand it as enny body   the rest of the recruits have not got here yet but we expect them every day to get here. I have wrote to Mother about the money that I sent by the Paymaster so that there is no use of writeing enny more about it I sent 80 dollars   he will send Father A check on the bank when he gets to Louisville. there is so many in here that I cant half write so I will not write enny more today. I will try and write some more before the mail goes out tomorrow so no more at present.

This from your brother
Ira

Nov 4th

every thing remains the same as usally. we have not receved enny more orders about moveing. some begin to think that we will not move.

Atlanta, Ga. Nov. 7th /64

Dear Parents

I will try and write a few lines to you today to let you know how I am getting along and where we are. I dont feel verry well at present the Doctor says that I have got A touch of the neuralga in my head and face but I am getting along very well now if I dont take any cold I will be all right again. the other boys are all well. the orders came for us to strike tents last Saturday and be ready to move immediately so we packed up our things and started marched out of the city in A south east direction went about two miles and camped for the night and was awoken early the next morning by picket fireing in front of us but it did not last long   there was one of our pickets killed and two wounded. there was about 30 of the Rebels all mounted and that afternoon we was ordered back to camp. we did not expect when we left that we was comming back into our old camp again. we remain under the same orders as before. some think we will move again before long. others think that we will not but we will not know much about it till we are ordered to pack up just as we did the other day. the rest of the recruits have not got here yet but they cannot be far off but they are driveing cattle so that they have to go slow. tell father to send me another diary so that it will get here by the commencement of another year. I received Catherines photograph all right and answered her letter the next day   I think it is A good one. I would like to have some photographs taken but there is no chance to get them here now. I cannot think of much to write today so I will close my letter for this time so that I can send it in this mail.

From your Son
Ira S. Jeffers

Atlanta Ga.
Nov 8th 1864

Dear Parents

We expect to leave here soon   we have just had orders to have our letters all in at the office at 7 o'clock and it is six now so I shall not have much time to write.   the Chaplin said it would be the last mail that we would probably have A chance to send in A long time   we are going to make A big move somewhere and it is not likely that we will have enny communications with the rest of the Army until we arrive at some other point.   I cannot form much of A idea where we are going and it would not do for me to write it if I did know at present.   I receved A letter from Fay Hope this afternoon but I have not got time to answer it   it is quite rainly weather now but we shall try to stand all bad weather if we only get enough to eat we will be satisfied.   it may be that there will be anouther chance to write and send letters if there is I will try and inform you of where I am.   I shall have to close now so no more at present.

From your Son
Ira

In the Trenches before
Savannah Ga. Dec. 18th 1864

Dear Parents
It is with pleasure that I embrace this opportunity of writeing A few lines to you. it is the first time that we have had A chance to send letters since we left Atlanta. we have not had enny communication until we arrived here. we got A mail yesterday I received two letters from you one dated the 7th and the other the 12th. I received Catherines Photograph all right before we left Atlanta and answered her letter. I was glad to hear that Father got my Vote in time to put it in. I sent it the day that I was 21. I received A letter from Amanda one from Frelia and Emiline the mail will not go out untill tuesday so I expect that if nothing happens I will have A chance to answer them and send them all in the same mail. we left Atlanta the 15th of Nov. we have had A prety hard march but met with but little oppisition on the part of the ennamy. we passed through Milledgeville the Capital of Georga it was not as large A town or as nice as some

Union soldiers voting

other towns in the state but it is quite place. the buildings are A great menny of them are quite old. that makes it look different. we are laying near Savannah River   there is only one Regiment between us and the River. we can see the City quite plain from the River Banks. the Rebel gunboats come up the River when it is high tide and shell us but they have not done much damage yet. our Brestworks are within in plain sight of the Rebel works   they throw A good manny shell at us. we have not used much artillery yet. where our Regiment is it is in such plain sight of the Rebel works that we cannot show our heads A great while at A time above the works. if they do they are in danger of getting hit. on our way through we had two men captured and since we got here we had one wounded in our company   I dont know just what the loss in the Regiment has been. Bob Winner is dead he died at Nashville Nov. 7th   the captain has had official notice of it. it will be sad news to his folks if they have not heard of it already but may the Lord support them in their offictions. when I saw Bob the last time I though that he would get well. that was what I wrote to you just before we left Atlanta. Milt and myself are well as usial. I may have A chance to write some more before the mailing.

Ira

Dec 19th/64

every thing is the same as usial this morning. I worked on A
fort nearly all night last night but I thought that I had rather
write some this morning then sleep for the mail is going out
at noon today whitch is sooner then we expected. we had
a man wounded in our company just before dark last night
he was shot through the fleashy part of the arm below the
elbow. but did not break enny of the bones. the rest of the
boys are all well as usial. when you write again Direct to the
137th regt NYSV
> 3rd Brigade
> 2nd Division
> 20th Army Corps
> Left wing Army of Georga

Savannah Ga.
Dec 25th 1864

Dear Parents

I will try and write A few lines to you to let you know that I am well and where we are. we are now in possession of the city of Savannah our Brigade was the first troops in the city so we are doing the Provost duty. I receved two letters from you while we lay outside of the city and answered them the mail had not come regular so that we knew not when to write until now but I shall try and write often now we have got good quarters our Regiment is quartered in A block of old stores not old stores but empty stores nice and built of brick. some of them are full of goods yet the Army did not destroy much of the things that was left here and nearly all of the citizens stayed here. there was none of the cotton distroyed it was all left here in good order and in A large amount to. besides A large amount of Rice and Molasses and Corn and A great many other Government stores and they left nearly all of their Artillery that they had in there works. there was not much fighting done to get the place not as much as we expected there would be. the Rebels are not far off now I expect they are just about on the other side of the river. I shall have to hurry up my writeing so as to get my dinner before I go on guard duty and I will not come off from guard untill the mail will go out so I will close for this time by wishing you all A Merry Christmas. wish you all A MERRY CHRISTMAS.

From your Son
Ira S Jeffers

1865

Campaign of the Carolinas January to April
Averysboro North Carolina, March 16
Battle of Bentonville, March 19 – 21
Occupation of Goldsboro, March 24
Advance on Raleigh, April 9 – 13
Occupation of Raleigh, April 14
Bennett's House, April 26
Surrender of Johnson and his Army
March to Washington, D.C., via Richmond Virginia, April 29 – May 19
The Grand Review, May 24
Veterans and Recruits transferred to the 102nd New York Infantry,
June 1
Regiment mustered out June 9

Savannah Ga.
Jan 3rd 1865

Dear Parents

I thought as I had time that I would try and write A few lines to you. it has been some time since I have had A letter from you but I expect that there is some on the way for me. I do not get my Republican enny more for some reason   if the subscription had run out tell Father to pay it again and have it directed to Co. F 137th Regt. N.Y.S.V. 3rd Birgader 2nd Division 20th Army Corps. I will send some Savannah papers in the same mail with this letter. they are the latest daily paper   I have sent him some before   he will probably get them some time before he does this one.

Jan 6th

I did not have time to finish my letter the day that I commenced it for I had to go on guard and have been on ever since I am guarding A wholesale Sutlers store. I am on post eight hours in 24 so I do not get much spare time but I should have tried and wrote sooner but I sent the papers so that you had all of the news that there was better than I could have wrote it. the boys are all well at present and I am well. I went to Church Sunday where there was women and children and lots of Girls it looked A good deal like home if I could serve out the rest of my term out here it would not seem A great while. it does not seem much more like war here than it would to be doing duty in the city of New York but I am in hopes that the war will be over before long. it dont seem as though it could last much longer. I shall have to stop writeing now if I get my letter out in this mail so no more at present.

From your Son
Ira S. Jeffers

Savannah Ga.
Jan 17th 1865

Dear Parents

I received your letter of the 2nd night before last but was on guard so that I did not have A verry good chance to write till today. we expect to leave here in A few days A part of our Corps has orders to start this morning we will probable go some time this week. it seems as though there is no other command that can take enny place but Sherman we have been nearly all over the Confederacy since we have been in the Western Department and if Charleston and Richmond is ever taken it is likely this army will have it to do. If A skirmish line can enter A fort I dont see why A line of Battle cannot. but Butler thought that he had rather have white men do it. I cannot tell where we are going but I think it is likely that we will go to Charleston. General Geary has been made Brenet Major Gen. our Colonel has gone home on A furlough so I cannot see him about the money now. but the money was to be Deposited in the National Bank of Binghamton. and is probably there whether the pay master wrote to you or not. the Recipt that I have is to be kept here so that if I do not get the money that I can go back to the Colonel for it and he will go to the Pay master. I will draw off A form of the Recipt so you can see it for your self.

Head Quarters 137th regt NYSV
Atlanta Ga. Oct 20th/64

$80. Received of Ira S Jeffers, Eighty dollar ($80) to be placed to the credit of Leverett Jeffers, at the Bank of Binghamton, NY.
Signed by the colonel
Commanding Regt.

I was told that the pay master would write to you that it was there and then you could drew it you will be likely to find there if you find it at all. And about Bob Winners money all that I can tell his folks is that he drew $(124) one hundred and twenty four dollars and he was sick in bed when he drew it so he could not have spent much. and as near as I can find out he was in debt to the boys in all about ten dollars whitch he paid. I have got to go to the Hospital now to see some of our boys that are there they are going to be sent to NY. and they want to see some of us before they go.

Savannah Ga.
January 19th 1865

Dear Parents

I will try and write A few lines to you again to let you know that I am well and so are the rest of the boys that you know. I have not had A letter from you since we took Savannah. I had two from you when we was in the breastworks before the city but have not had enny since I had one from Dell A few days ago we have not had enny mail but twice or three times since we have been here and then there was but A few letters for the Regiment. our letters leave Head Quarters but I dont know whether they go through or not. I cannot see why we cannot get mail here but there is probably some reason for it there is some talk of opening A recruiting office here for the Navy. they will take Soldiers that have served two years and enlist them in the Navy for 5 years I dont know just what the bounty is but it is over A $1,000 thousand dollars and they give them A furlough of about 60 days. there is A good many in our Regiment that say they intend to go as soon as they open the office so they can enlist I would liked to have went in the Navy when I had but two years to serve but I dont think I shall go now unless I can go for my unexpired term whitch is only about 8 months so I will not be very likely to go. I certainly shall not enlist for 5 years but there is some of the boys that say they will. I have got A song that I will send in this letter to Catherine it will show how patriotic the Southern Girls are. and there is A good many of them here in this city. the greater part of the people in the city want to come back into the Union but there is some old secessionist left. some of the boys have just come up from the dock and say that the mail boat has just come in if it has

I may get A letter if I do I will answer it inmediatly. I shall have to finish this so as to get it in the office to go in the first mail that leaves so no more at present.

From Ira

Savannah Ga.
Jan 20th 1865

Dear Parents

As I have time so that I can I will write A few lines to you so that you may know how I am getting along. we was relined from guard duty here in town yesterday and was ordered to be ready to march this morning as soon as the road was cleared of the other troops but it has rained so as to make the roads verry bad so that we have not got started yet. It will be two or three days yet. I think before we get away although we may go enny time. we was relined by the 19th Corps from the Army of the Potomac. we will be likely to go to Charleston or in that direction by land. It is not likely that we will have much of A chance to write letters or to sent them. so if you do not get enny letters from me in some time you will know the reason why. we have not had much mail come to us since we have been here. but I have wrote several letters you will get them after A while. we expect A mail this afternoon. they say its at Head Quarters now and will be to the regiment this evening. I will wait now till the mail comes. I will try and write some more then.

Jan 21st 1865

The mail did not get to the regiment till today. then I recived A letter from you with Alberts photograph and A letter from Uncle George one from Afrelia and Emiline one from Fray and Aunt Malaline. so I shall have something to do to answer them this afternoon. I think that Albert has grown A good deal since I left home. I should not have known him if it had not come in A letter from home. I have got me an Album to put all of my Photographs in so that I can keep them good. we do not know when we will move for it is raining all the time so that the roads are impassable for troops at present. I wrote to you in my last letter about the money. It probable is in the Bank of Binghamton and it is likely that the Pay Master has had so much to do that he has not notified you yet where it is. I have not got my Diary nor have not sent my old one home yet. I do not get my Republican enny more. I would like to have it sent for six months more if you can continual. I have got so many letters to answer this afternoon that I shall have to stop now. I will write to Catherine in A day or two.

Ira

Dear Sister

I will write A few lines to you today to let you know that we have not left Savannah although we expect to soon. the weather has been so bad that it has been impossible to move so large an army. I received A letter from Mother the other day with Alberts Photograph in it   also A few lines that you wrote. I think that you have improved A good deal in writeing lately. if you study all of the studys that you say you do I should not think that you could find much time to practice writeing. you wrote that you thought I must have got to be A big Bewhiskered fellow but you are greatly mistaken. I know that my father had plenty of Whiskers but I think I must take after my mother in that respect as she has none. I think the prospects are slim of my ever haveing enny. I have not married A Southern Belle yet but I will send you the Likeness of one and ask your advice on the subject as you may be A better judge of the fair sex that I am and it may be that you had rather have A sister in law of your choice. And as to the color you will be able to decern that from the Likeness without my telling you. you can tell the Girls at home that they need not to despair for there is A great chance for comming home A single man yet. although things may look <u>Dark</u> at preasant.

From your Brother Ira

you may want A lock of her hair but I think that you must be satisfied with the Likeness that is enough

A few words to Mother

Dear Parents

    we are about to start on another campaign and it probably will be so that I cannot write but few letters but I want you to write to me as often as you can for manny times we can get letters when we cannot send them and I want to hear from home as often as I can. I am well and healthy. the southern climate agrees with me first rate. I would have my likeness taken but they charge two dollars for it without enny case   I may have it taken yet before we go   if we do I will send it.

From your son Ira

Camp of the 137th Regt.
in the field near Fayetteville, N.C.
March 14th 1865

Dear Parents

I have another opportunity to write A few lines to you. It has been A long time since we have had A chance to send letters. I receved A letter from you the morning that we left Savannah after we was in the line ready to start and was glad to hear that you was all well. I am well at present my health has been very good ever since we started on this campaign we are now about two or three miles from Fayetteville we passed through there yesterday it is quite A large town. we have had some prety hard marching and some very bad swamps to go through and in one of them I seen an Alligator or Crocodile that some of the boys had killed. it was not A very large one it was about six feet long but it was large enough so that I could tell something how they look. I saw Norman Vance today he is well. Milt Knox is well and I think all of the other boys are that you know. we have not had mail yet we are in hopes that we will before we go we dont expect to stop here but A few days. I expect that it will be some time before we get through with this campaign and probably as soon as we leave here we will leave our communications again but I would like to hear from the United States once before we go. I think that the war will end this summer. I shall have to seal up my letter now for the mail is going out right away. I did not know as it was going as soon as it is. I will try and write again before we leave here so no more at present.

From your Son
Ira

Camp of the 137th Regt. NYV
near Goldsborough, N.C.
March 28th 1865

Dear Parents

We are in camp again for A short time and have the priviledge of writeing and sending letters and receiving letters. I received three letters from you yesterday. I was glad to hear that you was all well and that you had got my money all right. I am well at present and so are the rest of the boys that you know. the boys are all busy building tents but I have not got enny tent to put up at preasant. Jim Young was out foraging the other day and he had my tent and his on the horse for saddle blankets and the Rebel Cavalry got after them and Jims horse run into A fence and throwed him off and broke his arm and the Rebels went on past him. then he run into the woods and got away from them but he lost his horse and all the things but the Rebels caught five of the boys from our Regt. and three from our company. but there was none of them that you was acquainted with. Father knows Jim Young. He was the boy that worked at Foxes when he pulled stumps there. I have not wrote A letter in so long of time that I do not know how to go to work to do it. I will try and write A good long letter after we get settled down A little so that I can have A chance to think of enny thing. I have three or four more letters to answer but I shall not try to do it some days yet. I feel more like going to sleep then enny thing else. I got my papers in the mail yesterday but I have not had time to read them yet. I worked all day yesterday drawing stuff to build A tent for the Captain. The mail is just going.

Ira

Camp near Goldsboro, N.C.
March 30th 1865

Dear Parents

I have received three of four letters from you since we have been here. they came nearly all together for they could not get here before but they came just as acceptable as though they had come one by one in regular order. I have wrote one letter to you since we have been here but I did not have time to write much at this time   tell Father that I got my papers all right now   I have not read my papers much yet for I have had so much to do for the first few days fixing up our camp that what spare time I do get I use in writing.   I wrote A letter to Catherine today   I received one from her yesterday and one from Fay.   tell Father that I want him to take good care of the little Black Colts for if nothing happens to me I may want to drive them some next fall and winter   as to the winter here I have not seen snow enough this winter to amount to A good frost.   we have been having nice spring weather here for some time   the Plumb trees have been in full bloom here for over A week   it has rained nearly all day today but it has been A warm rain.   tell Grandma that I am well and enjoy my self as well as I can here in the Army. Elisha Bugdorf left us at Savannah and went to the Hospital and got back today   he looks as well as I have seen him in A long time   we do not expect to be here only about 30 days from the time that we stopped here.   we are getting clothed up as fast as they can get the clothing here   we was prety hard up for clothing when we got here for we did not get only half that we wanted after the Savannah campaign.   there was A good many of the boys that was barefooted when we got here and A good many of them had on half Rebel clothes   I wore out one pair of citizen pants but I want all blue while I am in the government service   after that I dont think that they will get enny thing but citizens clothes on to me   I think that the war must be about played out by this time. Lon Cronk from Port Crane was captured on the march by the Rebels while out forageing   there has been several of our men captured on this march when out forageing. I have about filled up my paper so I will close for this time.

From your son

Ira

Camp of the 137th regt. NYV
Near Goldsboro, N.C.
March 30th/65

Dear Sister

I recived A letter from you the other day dated Feb. 24th. I was glad to hear from you again and to hear that you was well. I am well at present   we are in camp again for A short time   we have had A long march but we are getting used to them. the boys are all well that you know. Lon Cronk from Port Crane was taken prisoner by the Rebels on this march he was in the 149th N Y   we have had several men Captured on this campaign   (3) three from our company   they were captured while out forageing. the rebs captured several beef cattle from us yesterday while they was outside of the picket line feeding. I was outside of the lines only A couple of days before about 12 miles A forageing and there was some men captured that day from some of the other detailes. they was skirmishing on the right and left of us and we made up our minds that it was time that we started for camp. I had A good mule and I made up my mind that they would have to do some traveling if they got hold of me and the reds was mounted too   I hope that you will get along well with your school and make the big boys and girls behave themselfs   I would like to visit your school but I am afraid that I would give you more trouble that all of the other sholars. if you have enny young Ladeys at your school give them my best respects and good wishes. I would like to know if Bekey Etehinson comes to school. you must tell frelia and Emiline that I will try and write to them in A few days. I several letters to write and will get around with them as fast as I can as it is a rainny day. I shall get A good start with them today tell dell that I got his picture all right and will have mine taken as soon as there is A chance for it. but there is not of A chance here in the army unless we stay in camp some time. I will now bring my letter to A close for you will have enough to do to read what I have wrote.

Ira

Camp of the 137th N.Y.S.V.
Near Goldsboro, N.C.
April 4th, 1865

Dear Parents

I received A letter from you this evening just as I was going to bed and as the officers are doing some writing and there is A chance for me to write on their table I will write my letter now for I will not have time in the morning before the mail will go out. I have wrote two or three letters to you since we have been in this camp and have had several from you for they all come at once but they was just as good as though they had just been writen. the letter I got tonight was dated March 12th   I was glad to hear that you was all well. I am well at preasant the boys are all well that you know. Jim Young got thrown from A horse while out forageing one day and had his arm broken   I have been out forageing A few times but I went well mounted so that if the rebs did get after me that I could give them A good race to get me. Lon Cronk was captured while out forageing   there has been A good menny men captured on this march while they was forageing   it has been the only way that we could get our living   we have seen some hard times for rations but for myself I have fared well on this march and had enough to eat all of the time. we are getting A plenty now while we are in camp   we expect to march again in A few days. we probable will go on towards Richmond   old Sherman will have to have A hand in taken that. I think that we have taken quite A round about since we left home   we started from Virginia and went nearly round the Confederate States and through them and now nearly back where we started from. I think that about September that the war will be over. our time will be out then at least and if I am alive and well will probable be home on my next Birthday where I hope there is no fighting or coutention. I dont think that Albert will want to call me old Tree Peck by that time it is A quarter past eleven now so I will not write enny more at preasant.

Ira

Camp of the 137th NYSV
Near Goldsboro, NC.
April 7th 1865

Dear Parents

I have just received A letter from you dated March 6th and was glad to hear that you was all well. I am well at preasant. we are haveing A spell of weather now. it seems like the month of June at home. the trees in the woods are all leaved out. and the plum trees are all in full bloom and have been for some time. we expect to start on another campain the first of next week. we have heard of the Capture of Richmond and Petersburg. there was considerable rejoyicing in the camp last night over the success of Grants army. there was one of the Officers of our Regiment just came from Division Head Quarters he says that prospects is that we will not move as soon as we was expecting to. but I will try and write just before we start at least. I should think that the Rebels would begin to get discouraged now that they have had to leave Richmond. I get my paper all right now. our mail comes now quite regular. there has been some changes in our Corps of Officers. the Corps is commanded now by General Mowry. he is one of the western Generals. I do not know what Corps he is from. our Colonel has got back he has been home on A leave of absence he left us at Savannah. his health has not been verry good for some time. there has not been enny verry high water here for we have not had enny snow or ice to melt. I seen A Binghamton Standard that had an account of high water you have. we are getting prety well clothed up again now. we was A hard looking lot of men when we first got here. there was A great menny entirety barefooted and some partely dressed in Reb clothes and some had full Rebel suits on. I wore out one pair of Reb pants. we had to wear them or go naked. but I dont think that we will see another such A campain as that one was. we will be so that we can get supplies from some Base as often as once A month probable. if do we can keep well clothed. we have to pay about double now for clothes to what we did last year. but I have got enough now to last me my time out if I dont have enny bad luck and take enny care of them. I sent you my Diary nearly A week ago but I have not wrote to you that I had sent it before. I did not keep it filled up on the Georgia Campain for I had all I could do to take care of myself. I have had good health the most of the time on this campain there was A spell when we was comeing through South Carolina through the swamps that I had the chills A few times but they did not amount to much. the most that troubles me is the heat. I have fill up my paper so I will close

> From your Son
> Ira

Camp of the 137th Regt. N.Y.S.V.
Near Goldsboro N.C.
April 9th 1865

Dear Parents

we have got orders to be ready to march in the morning at day light. so I thought that I would write A few lines to you so that if I do not get A chance to write again verry soon you will know the reason why I do not write. I am well at preasant. we are having verry pleasant weather now. it may be so that we can get letters on this march and may not. I do not know where we are going or in what direction. I do not think this campain will be A verry long one. we have got A paper with the full account of the takeing of Richmond and Petersburg. and since I have been writeing some of the officers have seen A Telagraph Dispatch from Gen. Grant to Gen. Sherman that he is closely following Gen. Lee and will as long as there is enny of his army left and tells him to push Johnson immediatly. we are getting good news all of the time. and I do not think that Johnson will give Sherman menny hard fights. the army is in exelent condition now. we have had A number of men come back to us since we have been here that have been in the Hospital ever since we left Stevenson Ala. Ed Elwell has come back he was wounded at Wauhatchie. he looks well an tough his wound has got well so that it does not trouble him. Milt Knox is well we have kept together so long that I am in hopes that we will be able to return home together. the mail has just come in and I got my papers but no letter the mail was mostly all papers today. I shall have to stop writeing now for I have got

A good deal to do to get ready to march in the morning. so no more at preasant. I will write again as soon as I can.

This From Your Son

Ira

April 15th 1865

Dear Parents

The mail is going out this afternoon so I will try and write A few lines to let you know how we are getting along and where we are. we got to Raleigh without enny fighting the trouble is we cannot get near enough to him to fight him we had official notice of Lees Surrender before we got here and we are expecting to hear of Johnsons Surrender before long. there is no use of his trying to hold out enny longer and I dont think that he will. we had orders to march this morning but it has rained so hard all day that we have not got started yet so we will not be likely to go till tomorrow. Jake Lewis is here within about A mile of where we are but I have not seen him.   the war is about over but we will probably not get home till our time is about out   but if the war will stop I will be satisfide to stay till my time is out. it is so rainey and wet that I cannot take enny comfort trying to write so I will close.

This from your son
Ira

HURRAH FOR THE UNION

Camp near Raleigh, N.C.
April 21th 1865

Dear Parents

I received A letter from you yesterday of the 7th of April and was glad to hear that you was all well. I am well and enjoying myself as well as ever. I have seen Jake Lewis and Charles Cole they are both well and send there best respects to all inquireing friends especilly Grandmother we are having all kinds of news. we have heard of the Assasination of President Lincoln. it is sorry news. the Rebel Army in these parts have all surrendered and there papers have been sent to Washington and if there papers are accepted we will be all right our General told us yesterday in A speech to the troops that we probably would not stay here more than ten days at the fartherest then we would march on near Washington and have one Grand review of the Army then each state would be sent to there state capital and be discharged. but I think that it will be all of 4 months before we get home. I shall begin to belive that this is coming to pass when I begin to see it. the army is all lying still and takeing it as cool as they can but the weather is terribale hot now but as long as we do not have to march I am satisfide. Milt Knox is well we have been together ever since we came into the service and we intend to try and come home together if nothing happens the mail has got so that it comes to us quite regular now so I want you to write often. I have writen one letter to you since we have been here I look for some more letters in the next mail. if we lay in camp A great while I shall not have much to do but write letters. it is getting so it almost A let down for the troops to keep still I get my paper every week now all right it is dinner time so I will close. we do not have as good liveing here as we did in Savannah   we cannot get enny thing but Army rations and not as much of that as we would like to. no more at present.

This from your son
Ira S. Jeffers

Camp near Raleigh, N.C.
April 28th 1865

Dear Parents

We have just had orders to have our letters in to the office at eleven o'clock tomorrow and that it is the last time that we will send A mail from here. we expect to start in A few days for Washington we marched out about 15 miles from here and stayed one day and came back today we went to hurry Johnson up to give him A chance to surrender or fight and the report is now that he has surrendered it was in the papers so today. we are going some where in A few days but we do not know where yet for certain there has been A leutenant just come here from the 76th N.Y. Battery he says that Johnson has surrendered and that the orders is at Corps Head Quarters for us to start to Washington A Sunday. there we will go into camp for A while we will probably get home sometime within the next two months but the WAR is over as near as I can learn. there is no use of my trying to write enny thing for it is all guess work and hear say. if I have A chance tomorrow and hear enny news I will try and write some more.

April 29th 1865

We have not had enny orders yet but we are prety sure that we will go tomorrow. we expect to march all of the way to Washington. there we will go into camp. until we are mustered out it will take some time to get around with all of the business to muster us out and settle accounts.

Ira

Camp Near Alexandra Va.
May 22th 1865

Dear Parents

I will try and write A few lines to you this morning to let you know that I am well and have not forgotten how to write if it has been A good while since I have wrote A letter. I wrote A letter to you when we was at Raleigh and we have not had A chance to send letters but twice or three times then, I did not know it soon enough to write. I had one letter from you when we was at Richmond and I got one from you yesterday and two papers from Binghamton. we have marched all the way from Raleigh here. And I expect that our marching is about over. there is some talk of our marching through to Baltamore. I seen Robert H. Spendly when we came through Richmond he said that he thought that he would get home in about one month from the time that I seen him he was well and looked as natural as ever. Sid Nowlan and Almeran Green are here they came to the Regiment yesterday. we are having A good menny men coming to the Regiment now from the Hospitals and other places they are anxious to get mustered out I expect that it will not be A great while before we will all be mustered out.

As today is Sunday the mail may not go out so I will not write enny more now and if it does go out today I will seal up what I have wrote so no more at present.

Ira

The Grand Review
May 23-24, 1865

On May 10th, 1865 President Andrew Johnson declares that all armed resistance was virtually at an end. Plans are made for the nation's capital to have the victorious Union Army march in the Grand Review. This would also bring Washington, D.C. out of its formal mourning period for the slain President Abraham Lincoln. On May 23rd – 24th, the victory parade will officially bring the brutal war to an end

General William Sherman's Army of The Cumberland, just finishing its 2,000 mile march through the heart of the Confederacy, arrived from North Carolina and camped around the Capital near general Meade's Army of the Potomac. Though the two armies camped on opposite sides of the river, the troops met up with one another in the taverns

Main reviewing stand
Pennsylvania Ave.

and brothels of Washington, D.C., where the customary rivalries led to numerous fistfights.

General Sherman, concerned that General Meade's army would outshine his own in the upcoming parade, ordered some last minute drilling and spit and polish sessions to whip his ragged troops into marching shape. General Sherman knew they could not match the close order discipline that General Meade's army perfected.

The parade's first day was devoted to General Meade's army, which was the capital's defending army. May 23 was a clear sunny day. Starting from Capitol Hill, the Army of the Potomac marched down Pennsylvania Avenue before virtually the entire population of Washington. Thousands were standing in the streets cheering and singing Union marching songs. At the reviewing stand, in front of the White House, were President Johnson, General Ulysses S. Grant, and other top government officials. Leading the day's march, General Meade dismounted in front of the reviewing stand and joined the dignitaries to watch the parade. His army made an awesome sight, 80,000 infantrymen marching 12 across with perfect precision. Hundreds of pieces of artillery and a line of cavalrymen that was seven miles long and took an hour to pass. Cavalry Officer George Armstrong Custer, gained the most attention that day, temporarily losing control of his horse when it became spooked, which caused some excitement as he rode past the reviewing stand.

The next day was General Sherman's turn. The march started at 9 A.M. on another beautiful day. His 65,000 man took nearly six hours to pass the reviewing stand with less precision than General Meade's forces, but they still thrilled the crowds anyway. Along with the sun browned, tattered, lean troops was a huge entourage that had followed General Sherman on his march to the sea. There were his medical workers, laborers, and his famous bummers who scavenged for the army's supplies. Plus his collection of livestock from the Carolina's and Georgia farm's, and following behind that were the black families who fled from slavery. Riding in front of his conquering force General Sherman later called the experience "the happiest and most satisfactory moment of my life."

After the war, General Sherman was commissioned Lieutenant General in the Regular Army, and after Grant was elected president, he promoted Sherman to the grade of full general and given command of the entire U. S. Army. He then retired 1888. General Meade mustered out of volunteer service, he continued in the regular army performing reconstruction duty in the South and was placed in command of the military districts on the east coast.

For the thousands of soldiers participating in the two day parade, it was one of their final military duties. Within a week of the Grand Review, the two main Union Armies were disbanded.

20th Corps marching down
Pennsylvania Ave.

Camp of the 137th NY
May 25th 1865

Dear Parents

I will try and write A few lines to you today to let you know where we are. we are Camped near the railroad between Washington and Annapolis Junction we are about 5 miles from Washington. Shermans Army was all reviewed yesterday in Washington. we expect to be sent to our different states soon to be discharged. I have heard that all of the '62 troops are to be mustered out as soon as possible but it will take some time to get all of the nessary papers made out and every thing turned over to the Government but it is some consolation to know that every time that we move that it is towards home. I think that we will be in Elmira in less than two weeks. then there will be some chance to get furloughs if we are not mustered out immediately. we will probably get mustered out so that we will get home by the first of July. the boys are all well and are so happy as clams in high water and I am in hopes that they will not be detained much longer in the service for they have been way from home A long time and have seen A good deal of rough usage. I would like to have the inhabitants of Binghamton see the old regiment what is left of it all together with out the recruits so they would see what there is left of over one thousand men that left there quite three years ago. we have had A good manny recruits besides one whole company since we have been out. Sid Nowlan and Almeran Green are well they are both in our company. I do not know whether they will be mustered out when we are or not. we have not been paid off since we left Atlanta and probably will not be until we get to Elmira. we may have to go to the State Capital to be discharged but

I dont think that we will   I dont see the need of that. I have not wrote menny letters for the last six months for we have not been where we could send them verry often and when we was half of the time we did not know it until it would be to late but if nothing happens now I shall be where I can write letters as often as I have A mind to. tell Grandmother that I am in hopes to be where she can see me herself before long. but tell her that I am afraid that she will not be able to keep me long at home for there is so many chances to get into buisness.

Ira

Camp near Alexandera, Va.
May 27th 1865

Dear Parents

I will try and write A few lines to you this morning to let you know that I am well and have not forgotten how to write if it has been A good while since I have wrote A letter. I wrote A letter to you when we was at Raleigh and we have not had A chance to send letters but twice or three times then I did not know it soon enough to write   I had one letter from you when we was at Richmond and I got one from you yesterday and two papers from Binghamton. we have marched all of the way from Raleigh to here   I expect that our marching is about over   there is some talk of our marching through to Baltamore. I seen Robert H. Spendly when we came through Richmond   he said that he thought that he would get home in about one month from the time that I seen him   he was well and looked as natural as ever   Sid Nowlan and Almeran Green are here   they came to the Regiment yesterday. we are having A good many men coming to the Regiment now from the Hospital and other places   they are anxious to get mustered out. I expect that it will not be A great while before we will all be mustered out. as today is Sunday the mail may not go out so I will not write enny more now and if it does go out today I will seal up what I have wrote so no more at present.

This from your son
Ira S. Jeffers

Camp of the 137th NY
May 28th 1865

Dear Sister

Your letter I receved the 20th but it was so cold and rainly that I could not write until today. it is verry pleasent today the sun comes out warm and is drying out the mud quite fast and I am in hopes that we will not have such A cold storm verry soon. our officers are making out the pay rolls now. we expect to get our pay this week unless they wait to pay us up in Elmira. if we go home by Elmira we will probably get home by the first of July but if we go by the way of New York and Albany we will not get home under two months. it will take some time to get mustered out at eather place. we expect to get mustered out of the United States here before we leave this place. we are camped within about 4 miles of Washington on the railroad. we were reviewed last wendsday in Washington. the troops are going home now as fast as they can discharge and pay them off. there will not be menny of this Regiment to Discharge if they do not Discharge the Recruits. but all of the 1862 troop are to be mustered out as soon as they can.

you must take your time to read this letter for it is not more than half wrote if you can read it at all you will do well. I am lying down to write on A blanket for I have not got enny thing to write on and as it is rather and uncomfortable way to write. I can not write A verry long letter. I am well and so are all the boys. there is but verry few sick in the regiment and I guess that they can sit up and eat their allowence of Government rations. no more at present.

From Your Brother
Ira

Soldiers returning home

Camp of the 137th NY
May 31, 1865

Dear Parents

As I have plenty of time to write and A plenty of material
for doing so I will write A few lines to you if I have not got
enny news to write. Every thing is quiet here in camp   we
do not have much of enny thing to do. camp guard is about
all of the duty. we have A plenty to eat such as it is. there is
but verry little sickness in the Regiment and what sick there
is they send to the Hospital and from there the most of them
are sent to there owen state or Discharged and sent home. as

for myself I am well and tough. and the other boys that you know are all well. I have never been away from the Regiment yet and so I am in hopes that nothing will happen that I will have to leave it until we are mustered out of Service in our owen state. we have not had enny orders yet but Officers are making out our papers as fast as they can. we expect to start as soon as the papers are done for the state. the Officers think that they will finish their papers by the first of next week. we will probably be mustered out of the United States Service here and turn over our Government property to the State of New York and be mustered out of the State Service there. It will take some time to get home after we get into New York State but I shall feel quite at home when we get into the state. I have been to Washington since we have been in camp here. I went through the Capital and the Patent Office. it would take A man two good months to go through the Patent Office and see all the patents and Relics and Presents from Foreign Countrys that have been Presented to the United States. the clothing that General Washington and Jackson used to wear are there besides A good manny other Relics of the Family of Washington. I cannot write much of interest so I will close my letter.

This From Your
Son
Ira S. Jeffers

Ira S. Jeffers was born on October 28th, 1843. Not much is know about his life before or after the war. He led a simple life in a small town called Port Crane, just outside of Binghamton, New York. In his family Ira was the oldest son. His father Leverett Jeffers was a farmer. His mother's name was Sophronia and he had a sister Catherine, and a brother Albert.

On September 25th of 1862 he answered the call of duty and enlisted in the 137th New York Volunteer Infantry. He served with the 137th New York throughout the War. Upon his discharged from the Army on June 9th 1865 he went back home to Port Crane, New York. Once home he met Georgianna Bullard and on February 22nd, 1866 they married at Whittneys Point, New York. A short time after their marriage they moved to Lone Tree, Nebraska, in Merrick County. On November 9th, 1871, Georgianna died of unknown causes at the young age of 22 years. After the death of Georgianna, Ira met Miss. Sarah L. Hollywood and on November 17th, 1872 just a year after the death of Georgianna he married Miss. Hollywood who was only 15 years old with Ira being the age of 29.

Sometime after their marriage, Ira and his young bride Sarah moved to Palo Michigan, where their first child is born. The child was a daughter named Ada and was born on July 24th, 1877. Shortly after Ada's birth Ira and his new family moved from Palo to Illinois. According to Illinois census records Ira, Sarah and Ada lived in Chicago during the 1880's, and Ira was working as a cabinet maker. Life was hard and work was not as plentiful as Ira had hoped. Ira and the family decided to move back to Michigan and back to the small town of Palo. Once back in Palo, Ira and Sarah where blessed with a second child, a son they named after his brother, Albert. Albert J. Jeffers was born on February 2nd, 1896. Now settled in Palo, Ira decided to open a Hardware store where he sold hardware, sporting goods, ammunition and guns. He ran his store until February 12th, 1907 when he applied for his pension from the Federal Government. At the age of 89, Ira died in his sleep on March 13th, 1932. On March 28th of that same year his wife Sarah applied to the Government for a Widow's Pension. Sarah went on to live another 10 years passing away on April 3rd, 1942 at the age of 85. Ira and Sarah are buried in the same plot with their son Albert, who died in 1970. Next to the family plot in Palo is Ira's father Leverett who died in September, 1885.

Undated photo of Ira and Sarah Jeffers
Palo, Michigan

STATE JOURNAL COMPANY, LINCOLN, NEB.

MARRIAGE LICENSE

The State of Nebraska, } ss.

Merrick _____ COUNTY, }

OFFICE OF THE COUNTY JUDGE

Affidavits from each of the contracting parties hereto having been taken and filed as required by law, License is hereby granted to any person authorized to solemnize marriages according to the laws of said State, to join in marriage

Mr. Ira S. Jeffers _____ and Miss Sarah L. Hollywood

of the County aforesaid, whose ages, residence, etc., are as follows:

NAMES OF PARTIES		Age	Color	Place of Birth	Residence	Father's Name	Mother's Maiden Name
Ira S. Jeffers	Groom	29	white	N. Y.	Lone Tree	Leverett Jeffers	Sophronia Schoffel
Sarah L. Hollywood	Bride	15	white	Mich.	Lone Tree	Thomas Hollywood	Lucinda Coon

And the person joining them in marriage is required to make due return of this License, together with the annexed Certificate, to the County Judge of the said County, within three months, of the names of the parties, time and place of marriage, and by whom solemnized.

In Testimony Whereof, I have hereunto set my hand and affixed the seal of the said Court, at my office in

[SEAL] Lone Tree _____ *in said County, this* 17th *day of* November *A. D.* xxxx 1872

John L. Martin

County Judge.

By _____

Clerk County Court.

CERTIFICATE OF MARRIAGE

To the County Judge of Merrick _____ County, Nebraska:

This Certifies, That on the 17th *day of* November *A. D.* 19xx 1872, *at* Residence of Judge Martin *in said County, according to law and by authority, I duly JOINED IN MARRIAGE, Mr.* Ira S. Jeffers *and Miss* Sarah L. Hollywood _____, *and there were present as witnesses* Jennie Hollywood

of _____ *County,* _____, *and* Calisle Carrier *of* _____ *County,* _____
(NAME OF COUNTY) (STATE)   (NAME OF COUNTY)   (STATE

Given under my hand the 17th *day of* November *A. D.* xxxx 1872   John L. Martin

350

DECLARATION FOR PENSION.

THE PENSION CERTIFICATE SHOULD NOT BE FORWARDED WITH THE APPLICATION.

State of _Michigan_
County of _Ionia_ } ss.

On this _12th_ day of _February_, A. D. one thousand nine hundred and _Seven_, personally appeared before me, a _Notary Public_ within and for the county and State aforesaid, _Ira S. Jeffers_, who, being duly sworn according to law, declares that he is _63_ years of age, and a resident of _Palo_ county of _Ionia_, State of _Michigan_; and that he is the identical person who was ENROLLED at _Camp Susquehannah, N.J._ under the name of _Ira S. Jeffers_, on the _20th_ day of _August_, 1862, as a _Private_, in _Company F, 137th Vol. Inf. N.Y.S. Vol._
(Here state rank, and company and regiment in the Army, or vessels if in the Navy.)
in the service of the United States, in the _Civil_ war, and was HONORABLY DISCHARGED
(State name of war, Civil or Mexican.)
at _near Bladensburg, Md._ on the _5th_ day of _June_, 1865.
That he also served _____
(Here give a complete statement of all other services, if any.)

That he was not employed in the military or naval service of the United States otherwise than as stated above. That his personal description at enlistment was as follows: Height, _5_ feet _6_ inches; complexion, _Dark_; color of eyes, _Blue_; color of hair, _Light_; that his occupation was _Farmer_; that he was born _in Port Crane, N.Y._, 1843, at _October 28th 1843_.

That his several places of residence since leaving the service have been as follows: _State of N.Y._ _certificate Nebraska, Illinois and Michigan._
(State date of each change, as nearly as possible.)

That he is _____ a pensioner. That he has _____ heretofore applied for pension _____ _Certificate No. 574,336._
(If a pensioner, the certificate number only need be given. If not, give the number of the former application, if one was made.)
That he makes this declaration for the purpose of being placed on the pension roll of the United States under the provisions of the act of February 6, 1907.
That his post-office address is _Palo_, county of _Ionia_
State of _Michigan_.

Attest: (1) _Thomas Wilkinson_   _Ira S. Jeffers_
(Claimant's signature in full.)
(2) _Geo Minier_

Also personally appeared _Ira S. Jeffers_ ~~Thomas Wilkinson~~, residing in _Palo Michigan_ and _Geo. Minier_, residing in _Palo_ _michigan_ persons whom I certify to be respectable and entitled to credit, and who, being by me duly sworn, say that they were present and saw _Ira S. Jeffers_, the claimant, sign his name (or make his mark) to the foregoing declaration; that they have every reason to believe, from the appearance of the claimant and their acquaintance with him of _30_ years and _30_ years, respectively, that he is the identical person he represents himself to be, and that they have no interest in the prosecution of this claim.

Validity accepted
S. A. Cuddy,   _Thomas Wilkinson_
Chief, Law Division.   _Geo Minier_
(Signature of witnesses.)
per J L H 25.

Subscribed and sworn to before me this _12_ day of _February_, A. D. 1907, and I hereby certify that the contents of the above declaration, etc., were fully made known and explained to the applicant and witnesses before swearing, including the words _at and certificate and Ira S. Jeffers_, erased, and the words _Thomas Wilkinson_, added; and that I have no interest, direct or indirect, in the prosecution of this claim.

[L. S.]   _John Galloway_

351

DECLARATION FOR WIDOW'S PENSION

ACT OF MAY 1, 1920, AND/OR JUNE 9, 1930.

State of _Michigan_, County of _Ionia_, ss:

On this _26th_ day of _March_, 1932, before me, the undersigned, personally appeared _Sarah L. Jeffus_ who makes the following declaration as an application for pension under the provisions of the act of Congress approved May 1, 1920, and/or June 9, 1930.

That she is _75_ years of age, that she was born _Aug 17th_, 1857, at _Black River, Michigan_.

That she is the widow of _Ira S. Jeffus_, who ENLISTED _Aug 20th_, 1862, at _Broome Co. N.Y._, under the name of _Ira S. Jeffus_ in _Co. 7 137 Ny Vol Regiment_

(Here state company and regiment, if in the Army; or vessel, if in the Navy)

and was honorably DISCHARGED _June 9th_, 1865, having served ninety days or more, or was discharged for, or died in service of the United States of a disability incurred in the service in the line of duty, during the CIVIL WAR, and who DIED _March 13th_, 1932, at _Palo Michigan_.

That he also served in _____

(Here give a complete statement of all other military or naval service, if any, at whatever time rendered)

and that, except as herein stated, said soldier (or sailor) was _____ employed in the military or naval service of the United States;

THAT SHE WAS MARRIED to said soldier (or sailor) _Nov 17th_, 1877, under the name of _Sarah L. Hollingwood_ at _Merrick Co. Nebraska_ by _John L. Martin, Judge of Probate_, that she had _not_ been previously married, that he had been previously married.

Ira S. Jeffus was married to Georgianna Bullard at Whitneys Point N.Y. on Apr 12th 1866 she died in Merrick Co. Nebraska Nov 9th 1871

(If there was a prior marriage of either, the name and the date and place of death or divorce of the former consort, or consorts, should be stated.)

That neither she nor said soldier was ever married otherwise than as stated above.

That she was NOT divorced from the soldier (or sailor) and that she has NOT remarried since his death;

That the following are the ONLY children OF THE SOLDIER (or sailor) who are now living and are under sixteen years of age:

(If he left no children under sixteen years of age, the claimant should so state.)

	born		at	_No Children_
	born		at	_under_
	born		at	_16 yrs_
	born		at	
	born		at	

That she _Did not_ serve in the Army, Navy, Marine Corps, or Coast Guard of the United States between April 6, 1917, and July 2, 1921, or at any time during said period.

(Did or did not)

That _a_ member of her family served in the Army, Navy, Marine Corps, or Coast Guard of the United States between April 6, 1917, and July 2, 1921, or at any time during said period. _Albert E. Jeffus (son)_

("a" or "no")

(If any members of claimant's family were in the military or naval service

77th infty 14th Division Headquarters Co. located at Camp Custer Battle Creek during the period mentioned, give the full name under which each such member served, with the designation of the organization in (or vessel on) which such service was rendered, together with the dates of enlistment and discharge. State also whether any such members are dead, and if so give the names.)

Enlisted Aug 27th 1918 at Ionia Co. Michigan discharged Jan 20th 1919

That she has _not_ heretofore applied for pension, the number of her former claim being _____; that said soldier (or sailor) was _____ A. a pensioner, the number of his pension certificate being _574336_.

That she hereby appoints _A. E. Nichols & Co._, _WASHINGTON, D.C._, her true

(Attorney) (Address)

and lawful attorney to prosecute this claim. AND FOR ACCRUED PENSION.

(1) _Ada J. Minier_

(Signature of first witness)

Sarah Nickison

(Address of first witness)

(2) _Esther L. Minier_

(Signature of second witness)

Palo Michigan

(Address of second witness)

Sarah L. Jeffus

(Claimant's signature in full)

Palo Mich

(Claimant's address in full)

Subscribed and sworn to before me this _26th_ day of _March_, 1932, and I hereby certify that the contents of the above declaration were fully made known and explained to the applicant before swearing, including the words _____ erased, and the words _____ added; and that I have no interest, direct or indirect, in the prosecution of this claim. _____

Ellis Bignell

(Signature)

Notary Public Ionia Co Mich

(Official character)

Palo Mich

(Post office address of officer)

My Commission Expires Dec 1, 1933

[L. S.]

Printed in the United States
121103LV00001B/190/P